Programming in Java

by

Mark Walmsley

BERNARD BABANI (publishing) LTD
THE GRAMPIANS
SHEPHERDS BUSH ROAD
LONDON W6 7NF
ENGLAND

PLEASE NOTE

Although every care has been taken with the production of this book to ensure that any projects, designs, modifications and/or programs, etc., contained herewith, operate in a correct and safe manner and also that any components specified are normally available in Great Britain, the Publishers and Author(s) do not accept responsibility in any way for the failure (including fault in design) of any project, design, modification or program to work correctly or for damage caused to any equipment that it may be connected to or used in conjunction with, or in respect of any other damage or injury that may be so caused, nor do the Publishers accept responsibility in any way for the failure to obtain specified components.

Notice is also given that if equipment that is still under warranty is modified in any way or used or connected with home-built equipment then that warranty may be void.

First Published – July 1998

British Library Cataloguing in Publication Data:

A catalogue record for this book is available from the British Library

ISBN 0 85934 436 3

Cover Design by Gregor Arthur
Cover Illustration by Adam Willis
Printed and Bound in Great Britain by Cox & Wyman Ltd, Reading

ABOUT THIS BOOK

This book provides an introduction to the Java programming language and the standard Java packages. The book is aimed at anyone interested in learning about Java and object oriented programming but it should be particularly useful for those wishing to rapidly acquire a good understanding of the Java language and start writing Java applets. No prior knowledge of Java is assumed although a general background in computing will be helpful — the presentation is pyramidal in structure with early chapters laying the foundations for those that follow. Each new concept is fully explained with the help of line-drawings and illustrative coding examples.

Following a general introduction in chapter 1 the book is divided into three parts:

I. Basic Language Features (chapters 2 to 4)
II. Advanced Language Features (chapters 5 to 10)
III. Standard Java Packages (chapters 11 to 14)

The first part discusses Java data types, expressions, statements and functions. Classes and interfaces form the basis for all object oriented facilities available in the Java language. The second part of the book covers object oriented topics such as initialization and finalization, object constructors, inheritance and packages — it also deals with arrays and the Java exception mechanism for structured error handling. The final part of the book provides an overview of the standard Java packages — java.lang and java.util, java.io, java.awt and java.awt.image, java.applet and java.net. The coverage throughout is broad rather than deep — many esoteric details are omitted for the sake of clarity.

All the code samples in the book have been compiled and tested under Microsoft's Visual J++ (version 1.1) — no Microsoft specific extensions are assumed and the software should work with any compiler conforming to the current standard for the Java language.

ABOUT THE AUTHOR

Mark Walmsley first discovered his interest in computing in the early 80s after reading a book on COBOL — he was soon writing programs in BASIC and shortly afterwards learnt about Z80 machine code. Over the last fifteen years he has gained considerable software development experience under both UNIX and Windows operating systems — he is familiar with a range of high-level languages (Pascal, FORTRAN, C, C++ and Java) as well as assembly language programming (principally for Z80 and 80x86 processors). Along the way he graduated first from Durham University and then from York University gaining degrees in Mathematics and Electronic Engineering — he eventually returned to Durham to study for a PhD in Computational Physics and there he was involved in developing simulation software for modelling electronic components. More recently his days are devoted to the twin pursuits of designing multi-player computer games and writing books on computer programming.

CONTENTS

1. Overview of Java

The Java programming language is object oriented in the tradition of C++ but there are some fundamental differences. In particular, Java programs are designed to be portable between different operating systems and in 'applet' form they may be embedded within Web pages. Java also smooths many of the rough edges of C++ and is not constrained by compatibility with C — for example, Java does not support pointers and relies on automatic garbage collection to reclaim unused memory. Nonetheless, Java has many similar features to C++ — both languages have a small number of intrinsic data types and programming constructs but complex data structures and processing algorithms can be built by combining the basic elements. Furthermore, C++ and Java each provide a plentiful supply of operators for data manipulation and they both use classes as the basis of their object oriented facilities. Each Java class defines a collection of objects all with similar characteristics, and every Java object belongs to some class. In addition Java defines the notion of an interface as a collection of related functions supported by an object. This chapter presents an overview of Java as an object oriented programming language, chapters 2 to 4 cover the basic language features and chapters 5 to 9 discuss Java classes and interfaces. Finally, chapters 10 to 15 describe the set of Java packages which contain the library of standard Java classes.

1.1 The Java Programming Language

Java is an object oriented programming language — the fundamental unit of a Java program is the 'class'. Each class defines a number of data fields together with a set of related functions to manipulate the data. A function consists of a sequence of program statements that are executed from top to bottom whenever the function is invoked. The Java language is free-format so that the text of the various statements may (with a few restrictions) be laid out in a fashion that best emphasizes the purpose of the code. In particular, extra spaces, blank lines and comments can be added where necessary — comments occur between matched /* and */ symbols or following // up to the end of the line. A semi-colon (;) is typically needed to mark the end of a statement — however, block statements are enclosed by { and } so that no terminating semi-colon is required.

Each program statement appearing within a class performs one of two basic operations:

1. To declare a data variable
2. To perform data processing

A variable declaration specifies the type of data held by the variable and allocates memory storage to hold the value of the variable. A variable defined within a function is a 'local variable' and it can be used only by that function — a variable defined by a class but not associated with a particular function is called a 'field' of the class. For example, an integer variable i may be declared as follows:

```
int i;
```

If i is a field the variable is initialized to zero — this is a common feature of Java for all built-in data types. On the other hand, if i is a local variable it must be explicitly initialized before it can be used in a data processing statement. In both cases the variable may be initialized as part of the declaration statement:

```
int i = 10;
```

Here i is assigned an initial value of 10. After a variable has been declared and initialized it can be used in a data processing statement. For example:

```
i = i+5;
```

In general the processing will change the value of the variable — however, fields declared as 'final' must be initialized when they are declared and remain constant thereafter.

For example:

```
final int TEN = 10;
```

Each Java class also defines a collection of functions to process its data. A function in Java is a modular piece of code which accepts data in the form of variables and constants, performs various calculations using these parameters and finally returns a result. For example, the following statement declares the `Telephone()` function as accepting a single parameter of type `String` and returning a **`long`** integer result:

```
long Telephone(String name) {
        .
        .
    // perform processing here
        .
        .
}
```

The function finds the telephone number associated with the `name` parameter passed to it — the telephone number is then returned as the value of the function. The return value may be used by the program statement which invoked the function — for example:

```
number = Telephone("MegaCorp");
```

This statement invokes the `Telephone()` function by passing it the string `"MegaCorp"` and the result returned by the function is stored in the `number` variable. The processing actually performed by the `Telephone()` function is defined by a sequence of program statements enclosed within the matching pair of braces `{ }`.

The Java language works with the `Unicode` character set. Each `Unicode` character is an unsigned 16-bit quantity — the first 128 values correspond to the 7-bit `ASCII` character set whilst a variety of languages from around the world are represented by higher character codes. To permit input using only `ASCII` characters, a general `Unicode` character can be denoted by a `Unicode` escape:

```
\uNNNN
```

where each `N` is a hexadecimal digit. A Java 'identifier' (or name) is composed of an unlimited number of letter or digit characters starting with a letter — here the underscore character (_) is considered to be a letter. Most Java code follows a standardized naming convention for classes, variables and functions. Classes (and interfaces) have names with the first letter of each word capitalized — function (and field) names are similar but they start with an initial small letter. For example, `String` and `PrintStream` are standard Java classes whilst `toString()` and `print()` are Java functions. Names for local variables and function parameters are typically short and use only small letters — single letter names indicating type (`i` for an **`int`** variable and so on) are also common. Finally, constants are written using capital letters and underscore characters — for example:

```
final int MIN_PRIORITY = 1;
```

Java reserves some identifiers as keywords and these keywords cannot be redefined by a program — the reserved list includes the following:

Intrinsic Data Types:
`boolean byte char double float int long short`

Data Processing:
`break case continue default do else for if switch while`

Fields and Functions:
`abstract final private protected public return static synchronized void`

Classes and Interfaces:
`abstract class extends final implements instanceof interface new public static super this`

Packages:
import package

Exceptions:
catch finally throw throws try

The introduction to the fundamentals of the Java language presented in this section is expanded in chapters 2 to 4. The next section discusses the use of Java classes in more detail and describes how they enable an object oriented programming style — further information on Java classes is provided in chapters 5 to 9.

1.2 Classes and Interfaces

In object oriented programming a problem is solved by identifying the essential ingredients of the problem and defining various object types (classes) to represent these concepts. The interaction of the objects then models the original problem and a solution may be expressed in natural terms. As discussed in the previous section each Java class defines two sets of elements:

1. Data fields
2. Functions for processing this data

A Java class provides a blue-print for generating a whole set of objects all with the same basic characteristics — thus Java objects do not occur individually but each one belongs to a particular class. An object can be created in much the same way as a variable of an intrinsic type — for example:

```
int i = 10;
String s = "Hello";
```

Here a variable of intrinsic type `int` and an object of class `String` are declared and initialized. However, for objects the **new** keyword is usually required — Java allows the short-hand notation shown above only for strings and the explicit version is:

```
String s = new String("Hello");
```

The functions supported by the `String` object can be invoked using the dot operator (.) as follows:

```
char c = s.charAt(0);
```

This statement assigns the character (`'H'`) at position `0` in the `String` object `s` to the character variable `c` using the `String` class function `chatAt()`.

All objects from the same class share the code which defines their functionality — the various objects are distinguished from each other by their own personal data fields. In general, an object's data is not shared by other objects of the class — however, the class may define additional data fields which belong to the class as a whole rather than to individual objects. Hence, a Java object is associated with:

1. Personal data fields
2. Function code shared with other objects of the class

These two elements should be viewed as internal to the object so that the implementation details are hidden from the outside world — this notion is known as 'encapsulation'. Of course, a program must be able to send requests to an object and the object may want to acknowledge these requests. The solution is to provide a well-defined communications interface for passing messages to and from the object. As long as the program makes requests through the interface and leaves the internal processing to the object, encapsulation is guaranteed. In Java an interface is implemented as a series of functions and requests are sent to an object by invoking the appropriate functions. An interface can be defined independently of a class simply by listing the set of functions supported by the interface — the interface specification defines the types of the function parameters and return values but not the processing performed by the functions. The details are covered in chapters 4 and 5 but the following figure demonstrates the essential ideas:

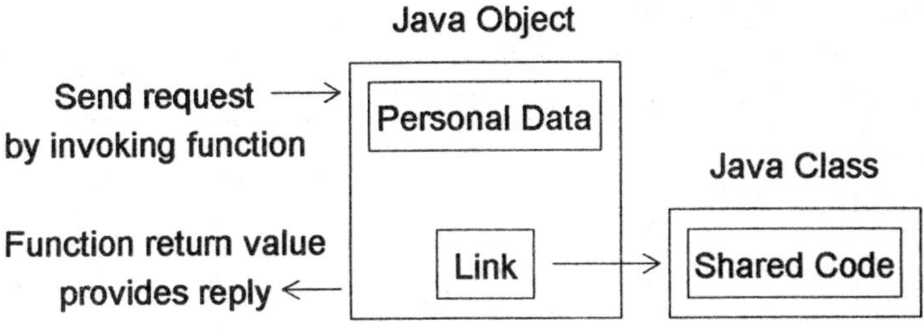

The benefit of encapsulating object implementation details and instead communicating through an interface is that code is modularised and interdependencies are reduced. Indeed one object may be substituted for another as long as they both support the same interface — this is the fundamental concept of 'polymorphism'.

1.3 Building a Java Program

The construction of a Java program can be quite a complicated business so it is important to understand the three main steps involved. Each of these steps uses a different tool:

1. Editor
2. Compiler
3. Virtual Machine

The editor is used to produce the text files containing the Java source code. These files are fed to the compiler which checks them for errors in syntax and (assuming all is well) proceeds to convert them into class files — these contain a set of basic machine-independent instructions known as 'byte code'. Finally, the Java Virtual Machine interprets the contents of the class files and performs the processing necessary to execute the Java program — the Java Virtual Machine provides a hypothetical standardized operating system on which to run Java programs. This approach has a number of advantages:

1. Java code is able to run on a wide range of real operating systems

2. Executable file size is reduced by relying on library code

3. Security can be improved by checking class files before execution

The whole process is illustrated in the following figure:

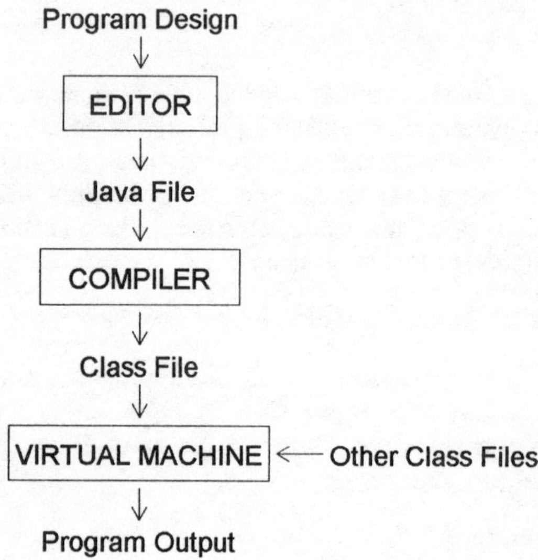

To speed up the final step the byte code can be converted on-the-fly to native machine code which is then executed directly on the underlying operating system.

The filenames of Java source and class files commonly end with the following extensions:

source file: `.java`
class file: `.class`

The filenames themselves are taken from the Java classes which the files contain. Consequently each file generally defines a single class — extra classes can be added to the file but they should only be used internally and do not influence the filename. A set of related classes may be arranged into a 'package' — the associated files are typically placed in a directory named after the package. Java provides a number of standard packages which define many features of the Java language — indeed the classes from the `java.lang` package are automatically available to all Java programs. Chapter 10 discusses Java packages in more detail.

1.4 The `Hello` Program

No-one is really happy with a new programming language until they have produced a `Hello` program using it — for Java this milestone is now in sight. Every Java program must contain the definition of a function called `main()` within some specified class and this function performs all the processing for the program — chapter 14 introduces an alternative approach based on 'applets'. When a Java program is run control transfers to its `main()` function — the name of the class containing the function is typically passed to the Java Virtual Machine as a command line parameter. The following program prints `Hello!` on the screen:

```
class Hello {
  public static void main(String[] params) {
    System.out.println("Hello!");
  }
}
```

This is a small program but there are lots of things to understand. Firstly, the format of the `main()` function is specified by the Java language itself. The function must be declared using the keywords **`public`**, **`static`** and **`void`** — the **`void`** keyword indicates that the function returns no result and the other keywords are explained in later chapters. The `main()` function should also be defined as accepting an array of `String` objects — each string corresponds to a parameter from the command line. The message `Hello!` is provided as a character string literal which must be enclosed in double quotes — the message is printed by the program statement:

```
System.out.println("Hello!");
```

The `System` class provides a standardized representation of the underlying operating system — the `out` field is defined by the `System` class and it corresponds to the standard output device which is usually the screen. The `out` object belongs to the `PrintStream` class and this provides `print()` and `println()` functions to print variables and constants of common types in readable form — the `println()` version appends a newline character `'\n'` to the characters printed. To run the program the class name `Hello` should be passed as a command line parameter — subsequent parameters appear as elements of the `params` array of `String` objects.

1.5 Summary

Java is an object oriented programming language — a Java program is built from a collection of classes that may be organized into packages. Each class defines a template from which a number of objects with similar characteristics may be created — an object contains its own personal data but shares function code with other objects in the class. A class is defined by specifying the data fields and functions belonging to the class — each function consists of a series of program statements that determine the processing which the class can perform. A set of related functions may be grouped together as an interface — an interface does not define the implementation of the functions. The Java language works with characters from the Unicode character set — identifiers (names) are constructed from a sequence of Unicode letters and digits starting with a letter. Certain identifiers are reserved by Java as keywords — these include keywords for (i) intrinsic data types, (ii) fields, functions and data processing, (iii) classes, interfaces and packages, and (iv) exceptions. The source code for a Java program is typically placed in files with a `.java` extension — these files are compiled into Java byte code stored in files with a `.class` extension. The byte code is interpreted by a Java Virtual Machine that actually performs the processing necessary to execute the Java program — the use of a Virtual Machine improves portability, security and reduces executable file size. When a program is started control passes to the `main()` function defined in a class specified on the command line — an alternative method of program execution involves the `Applet` class.

2. Expressions

Chapter 1 introduced the notion of Java data types — there are both intrinsic Java data types defined by the language and also object types (classes) which come from the standard libraries or are defined by the user. Java supplies only a few intrinsic types but provides a wide range of built-in operators to manipulate data of these types. This chapter details the intrinsic Java types and shows how data may be processed using expressions that apply the various Java operators. Indeed there are many kinds of expressions in Java (arithmetic, assignment, comparison, logical and bitwise) but each one is considered here in some detail. The chapter concludes with an overview of the input/output mechanism provided by the standard stream objects (`in` and `out`) — the library class `String` (used to represent sequences of characters) is also discussed.

2.1 Intrinsic Data Types

The Java language only defines a small number of intrinsic data types:

`char` — character type
`byte`, **`short`**, **`int`**, **`long`** — integer types
`float`, **`double`** — floating-point types
`boolean` — logical type

The size of a variable (in bits) for each particular type is standardized. Characters in Java are taken from the `Unicode` character set — each character is an unsigned 16-bit quantity. The numeric types (integer and floating-point) are all signed. For integers the variable sizes are 8, 16, 32 and 64 bits for **`byte`**, **`short`**, **`int`** and **`long`** variables respectively. The **`float`** and **`double`** types represent 32-bit single precision and 64-bit double precision floating-point numbers (as defined by an `IEEE` standard).

A character variable is used to hold a single text character (letter `a-z` or `A-Z`, digit `0-9`, punctuation mark, space, etc.) and a character value is denoted by enclosing the character within single quotes `' '`. For example:

```
char letter = 'a';
```

The Java characters are taken from the `Unicode` character set — the first 128 characters are identical to the 7-bit `ASCII` characters. An escape sequence of the form:

```
\uNNNN
```

where `N` is a hexadecimal digit (`0123456789ABCDEF`) may appear anywhere within the program — it specifies the character code of a `Unicode` character. For example:

```
char letter = '\u0061';
```

This performs exactly the same action as the previous declaration since the character code `\u0061` corresponds to the letter `a`.

A collection of characters forms a string and a character string constant is written within double quotes `" "`. In Java each string constant is associated with a `String` object — section 2.8 discusses the `String` class in more detail. The program in chapter 1 passed the character string `"Hello!"` to the `println()` function to display the message on the screen. The `println()` function adds a newline character to the end of the string — an alternative approach is to include the escape sequence `\n` (newline) explicitly in a call to the `print()` function. All the Java character escape sequences start with a backslash `\` and they each represent a single character that cannot be typed directly such as newline (`\n`), tab (`\t`) or formfeed (`\f`) — the backslash, single and double quote characters may be similarly escaped.

An integer variable can be of type **`byte`**, **`short`**, **`int`** or **`long`** and holds a whole number such as `-1000`, `0` or `33`. Both positive and negative values are possible and the range of values that the variable can hold is determined by the number of available bits — for example, a **`byte`** variable covers the range from -128 to 127. The MIN_VALUE and MAX_VALUE fields of the Integer and Long classes are set to the extreme values for **int** and **long** variables. Integer constants can be written in decimal, octal (starting with the digit 0) or hexadecimal (using the 0x prefix). All integer constants are of type **int** unless they include the suffix L (or l) which denotes type **long** — however, if a constant expression of type **int** is sufficiently small it can be stored directly in a **byte**, **short** or **char** variable:

```
byte b = 10;
```

Variables of type **float** and **double** hold the values of real numbers such as 3.14, 0.001 or 25E+25 which may include a fractional part. The letter E (or e) is used to express floating-point numbers in scientific notation — floating-point constants are assumed to be of type **double** unless the letter F (or f) is appended to specify type **float**. The range of values which a floating-point variable can hold are available from the MIN_VALUE and MAX_VALUE fields of the Float and Double classes. Very few computational errors involving numeric types cause a Java program to stop — for example, integer overflow simply truncates the result and floating-point overflow or underflow results in (positive or negative) infinity or zero respectively. The main exception to the rule is that integer division by zero will abruptly terminate execution.

Sometimes it may be necessary to convert from one type to another — this can be achieved by using a cast as follows:

```
int i;
float f = 2.5F;
i = (int)f;
```

The value of the **float** expression is converted (cast) to an integer type by discarding the fractional part. The cast ensures that the compiler does not object to the assignment statement — if the conversion were made automatically (without the cast) important information may be lost. Similar conversions between other numeric types are possible by specifying the appropriate data type in the cast statement. In addition Java performs implicit casts in a variety of situations. For example, **byte**, **char** or **short** values are routinely converted to **int** type before any calculations are performed — this is true even for the numeric unary operators (+, -, ++, -- and ~) which act on a single value. With the binary operators for arithmetic (+, -, *, / and %), comparison (<, >, <=, >=, == and !=) and also bitwise (&, | and ^) operations the two operands are cast to **int** (or **long**) type for integer calculations and to **float** (or **double**) type for floating-point calculations — the types **long** and **double** are chosen only if one of the operands already belongs to these higher precision types. Mixing integers and floating-point values results in a floating-point calculation.

Variables of the **boolean** type hold logical values — the only two possible values are `true` and `false`. For example:

```
boolean okay = true;
```

Boolean variables and expressions are particularly useful for controlling the actions of the various programming statements available in Java — chapter 3 covers this topic in detail. Note that it is not possible to convert directly between **boolean** and numeric types either explicitly or implicitly (as in C/C++). However, there are alternatives — for example:

```
boolean okay = (i != 0);
```

Here the variable `okay` is set to `true` unless the integer `i` is zero — neither `i` nor `(boolean)i` may be substituted for the `(i!=0)` expression.

There have already been several examples of a variable declaration statement. This consists of a type name followed by a variable name. Sufficient storage space is allocated to the variable to hold a value of the specified type — for character and numeric fields belonging to a Java class the variable is initialized to zero. A slight variation of the declaration statement includes an equals sign followed by a value — in this case, the variable is initialized to hold the given value. For example:

```
int count = 10;
```

This allocates storage for the `count` variable and initializes it with the value `10`. If a field variable holds a constant value it should be declared using the **`final`** keyword and an initialization value must be supplied:

```
final int TEN = 10;
```

Finally, several variables of the same type may be declared in a single statement by using commas to separate the individual variable names:

```
int count, sum, total;
```

2.2 Expressions

Most data processing in Java is performed using expressions. An expression is formed by combining constants, variables and objects with various operators. In general, expressions are calculated from left to right with operands being fully evaluated before they are combined by the operators — if an error occurs then the following steps in the calculation are not performed. One expression can be combined within another as a sub-expression and parentheses `( )` may be used to ensure the correct order of evaluation. For example:

```
answer = 9*(2+4);
```

Every Java expression has an effect and a result. The result is simply the value produced by the expression whilst the effect is something that happens because the expression is evaluated. Many expressions have no noticeable effect — however, those that do include the assignment expressions,

expressions involving the increment/decrement operators (++ and --) and expressions which invoke functions.

2.3 Arithmetic Expressions

Arithmetic operators are defined for the integer and floating-point types. There are unary operators which act on a single operand and binary operators which combine a pair of operands. For example, the unary minus operator can be used to negate a value:

```
five = 5;
answer = -five;
```

Here the `answer` variable is assigned a value of `-5`. The binary operators are `+` (add), `-` (subtract), `*` (multiply), `/` (divide) and `%` (remainder). For example:

```
six = 6;
seven = 7;
answer = six*seven;
```

Here the answer `42` is generated. The `%` operator yields the remainder after dividing one integer by another — for example, the following statement initializes the `answer` variable with the value `3`:

```
int answer = 15 % 6;
```

As noted in the previous section, the unary operators will extend a **`byte`**, **`short`** or **`char`** variable to type **`int`** before performing the operation — for binary operators the operands are converted to **`int`**, **`long`**, **`float`** or **`double`** type as appropriate.

The most interesting arithmetic operators are the unary operators `++` (increment) and `--` (decrement) which respectively increase or decrease the value of a numeric variable by `1`. For example:

```
count = 3;
count++;
```

The second statement increments the value of count to 4. As well as this effect of altering the value of a variable, the increment/decrement operators also produce an expression result which may be used within a larger expression. The result of the increment/decrement sub-expression is the value of the variable either before or after it is modified — the choice depends on whether the operator is placed to the right (postfix) or left (prefix) of the variable name. For example:

```
count = 3;
answer = 5 * count++;
```

The processing steps performed by the second statement are as follows:

1. The count++ expression yields the result 3
2. Since the ++ operator follows its count operand, the variable's value is incremented to 4 only after the result of the sub-expression is generated
3. 5 is multiplied by 3 to give the answer 15

By contrast, the following statements use the prefix form of the operator:

```
count = 3;
answer = 5 * ++count;
```

Again the value of count is set to 4 but now the value of answer is 20.

2.4 Assignment Expressions

The ++ and -- operators provide expressions with an effect and a result. The various assignment operators (=, +=, *= and so on) also do this. The basic assignment operator = simply assigns a value to a variable appearing on the left-hand side of the equals sign — this is the effect of the assignment expression. However, the assignment expression also produces a result which is the value assigned to the variable. The most common use is to chain together assignments which are then executed from right to left. For example:

```
int row, column;
row = column = 0;
```

The chained assignment expression performs the following processing:

1. The value of zero is assigned to the `column` variable
2. The sub-expression `column = 0` yields the value zero
3. The other assignment is then effectively `row = 0`

The overall effect is that both `row` and `column` variables are assigned the value `0`.

The other types of assignment operator combine the basic assignment operation with an arithmetic (or bitwise) operation. For example:

```
total += count;
```

This expression adds the value of `count` to the current value of `total` and then stores the result in the `total` variable as its new value. Each combined assignment operator implicitly casts the result of the expression to the type of variable on the left-hand side before storing it — in particular, if the variables `total` and `count` are of type **`byte`**, **`short`** or **`char`** then the calculations are performed using **`int`** values (yielding a result also of type **`int`**) but this is cast to the type of `total` before the final assignment. Furthermore, the value of the left-hand side is calculated first and saved whilst the right-hand side is evaluated — for example, the following statements eventually assign the value `3` (not `4`) to the `i` variable:

```
i = 1;
i += (i = 2);
```

The other combined assignments operators are the arithmetic operators `-=`, `*=`, `/=` and `%=` and the bitwise operators `&=`, `|=`, `^=`, `<<=`, `>>=` and `>>>=`. Section 2.7 describes the bitwise operators.

2.5 Comparison Expressions

Comparison expressions test a pair of operands for equality, inequality or relative ordering (less than, greater than, etc.) by using the following operators:

== equal to	!= not equal to
< less than	<= less than or equal to
> greater than	>= greater than or equal to

Do not confuse the assignment operator (=) with the equality operator (==). A comparison expression yields a logical result of type **boolean** — the value of the expression may either be `true` or `false`. Some examples of comparison expressions are shown below — the variables `six` and `seven` are assumed to hold the values `6` and `7` respectively.

```
six == seven (false)
six != seven (true)
six < seven  (true)
six >= seven (false)
```

The **boolean** result of a comparison expression may be further combined in a logical expression as discussed in the next section — both comparison and logical expressions typically appear as part of the Java programming constructs described in chapter 3.

2.6 Logical Expressions

Logical expressions process the **boolean** values `true` and `false`. The logical operators are:

`&`, `&&` and
`|`, `||` or
`^` exclusive or (xor)
`!` not

Except for the `!` (not) operator these are all binary operators and so take two operands. The 'and' operators `&` and `&&` yield true if and only if both operands are `true`. On the other hand, the 'or' operators `|` and `||` yield `true` if either the first or the second operand is `true` — they yield `false` only if both operands are `false`. The difference between the `&` and `|` operators and the `&&` and `||` operators is that the latter pair are short-circuit operators. This means that the left-hand operand is always evaluated but the right-hand operand is evaluated only if the evaluation is necessary to determine the overall result of the logical expression — the `&` and `|` operators always evaluate both operands. Hence for the `&&` (and) operator the procedure is:

1. Evaluate the left-hand operand
2. If it is `false`, return `false` as the expression's result
3. Otherwise evaluate the right-hand operand
4. Return the result of the expression

The procedure for the `||` (or) operator is similar.

For example, suppose the variables `five`, `six` and `seven` have the values `5`, `6` and `7` respectively in the following logical expression:

```
(five < six) && (six < seven)
```

Then the expression evaluates both of its operands and generates the result `true`.

The 'xor' operator `^` produces the result `true` if exactly one of the operands is `true` (but not both). Hence, continuing the previous example:

```
(five < six) | (six < seven)
(five < six) ^ (six < seven)
```

Here the first expression is `true` but the second expression is `false`. The `!` (not) operator changes `true` to `false` and `false` to `true` — following the assignments `black=0` and `white=1` the logical expression:

```
!(black == white)
```

yields the value `true`.

Finally, the ternary operator `?:` takes a logical expression as its first operand and depending whether this is `true` or `false` the operator proceeds to evaluate either its second or third operand (but not both) with the result being available for use in any containing expression. The type of the result is converted to **`int`**, **`long`**, **`float`** or **`double`** according to the types of the second and third operands — however, if one operand is a **`byte`**, **`short`** or **`char`** and the other operand is a constant **`int`** expression of sufficiently small magnitude then the smaller type is used. The ternary operator `?:` may be used as follows:

```
six = 6;
seven = 7;
smaller = (six < seven) ? six : seven;
```

Here the variable `six` is tested against the variable `seven` and since `six` holds a smaller value than `seven`, the variable `smaller` is assigned the value `6`.

2.7 Bitwise Expressions

The bitwise operators `&` (and), `|` (or) and `^` (xor) combine integer values one bit at a time. For each bit position the result of these operations is defined by the following tables:

& (and) operator

	0	1
0	0	0
1	0	1

| (or) operator

	0	1
0	0	1
1	1	1

^ (xor) operator

	0	1
0	0	1
1	1	0

The following code demonstrates the effect of the bitwise

operators:

```
three = 3;
nine = 9;
one = three & nine;
ten = three ^ nine;
eleven = three | nine;
```

The variables one , ten and eleven are assigned the values 1 , 10 and 11 respectively. The unary bitwise operator ~ (not) swops bits from 0 to 1 and from 1 to 0. Bitwise expressions are typically used with flag variables where each bit of an integer acts as a flag to indicate whether or not some option is enabled. For example:

```
int flags = MATH_COPROCESSOR|MEMORY_CACHE;
```

This sets the appropriate bits in the flags variable to select the desired options.

The two bit-shift operators << and >> move the bits in an integer variable respectively to the left (doubling its value) or to the right (halving its value) — the number of shifts is determined by the operator's second parameter. The >>> operator is similar to the >> operator but it shifts zeroes into the most significant bit position (sign bit) whereas the >> operator maintains the sign bit. For example:

```
three = 3;
twelve = three << 2;
```

2.8 Streams and Strings

The Hello program in chapter 1 introduced the notion of performing input/output with data streams and used the out output stream object to display a string on the screen — there is naturally a corresponding input stream object called in for reading data in from the keyboard. The two streams in and out are available as fields of the System class — they belong to the InputStream and PrintStream classes respectively but it is common to convert the in stream to a DataInputStream object to permit formatted input. The `DataInputStream` and `PrintStream` classes provide the `readLine()` and `println()` functions for performing simple input/output on a line-by-line basis. For example:

```
System.out.println("Enter password ...");
DataInputStream data =
  new DataInputStream(System.in);
String password = data.readLine();
```

This code prints the message `Enter password ...` on the screen and then creates the `data` stream to read in the `password` string from the keyboard.

Strings are used throughout a Java program to represent sequences of `Unicode` characters — in particular, each string constant appearing in a program is automatically associated with a `String` object. The string concatenation operator + can be used to join together two strings (either constants or objects) — for example:

```
String good = new String("Good");
System.out.println(good + "bye");
```

The string concatenation operator also works when one of the operands is of an intrinsic type such as **`int`** — in this case a string represention of the operand is generated before concatenation:

```
int k = 123;
System.out.println("k = " + k);
```

Furthermore, if a string is concatenated with an object from another class then the `toString()` function of the object supplies the string to concatenate:

```
System.out.println("It's " + new Date());
```

Here the `Date` object provides a string representing the current date and time. Finally, the assignment operator += acts as a string concatenation operator whenever the left-hand operand is a string — for example:

```
String s = new String("Hel");
s += "p!";
System.out.println(s);
```

2.9 Finding the Average

The following program demonstrates some of the ideas from this chapter. It reads in a pair of integers and stores them in the variables `i` and `j` — the average is computed and the result is printed out.

```
import java.io.*;

public class Application {
  public static void main(String[] params)
              throws IOException {
    int i,j;
    double x;
    DataInputStream data =
      new DataInputStream(System.in);
    System.out.println("First integer?");
    i = Integer.parseInt(data.readLine());
    System.out.println("Second integer?");
    j = Integer.parseInt(data.readLine());
    x = 0.5*(i+j);
    System.out.println("Average = " + x);
  }
}
```

When this program is run the following text appears on the screen:

```
First integer?
3
Second integer?
6
Average = 4.5
```

Note that the input values (3 and 6) are automatically echoed to the screen as they are typed. The `DataInputStream` class `readLine()` function inputs each value as a String object and the Integer class parseInt() function then converts the string to an integer. The **import** statement for the java.io package is needed to permit reference to the DataInputStream class using its simple name — chapter 10 discusses Java packages and importing of classes and interfaces. If the readLine() function encounters an error then it halts execution with an IOException error and the **throws** keyword in the declaration of the main() function is used to indicate this fact. Chapter 9 deals with exception classes such as IOException in much more detail — however, note here that the PrintStream class never generates an IOException error but instead sets an internal error flag.

The expression statement that performs the actual averaging computation is:

```
x = 0.5*(i+j);
```

Multiplication by the floating-point constant 0.5 ensures that the sum i+j is converted to a floating-point value before the average is calculated — dividing by the integer 2 would perform an integer calculation with the resulting value 4. An alternate method is to use an explicit type cast:

```
x = (float)(i+j)/2;
```

In any binary operation involving an integer and a floating-point value, the integer is converted to a floating-point number before the two values are combined.

2.10 Summary

The Java language only supports a few intrinsic types — there are integer types (**byte**, **short**, **int** and **long**), floating-point types (**float** and **double**), a character type (**char**) and a logical type (**boolean**). Nonetheless, there is a plentiful supply of operators for combining constants and variables of these types into quite complicated expressions. The arithmetic operators provide the usual add, subtract, multiply and divide operations — there are also prefix and postfix forms of the increment and decrement operators which change the value of a variable by one. In addition to the basic assignment operator for storing a value into a variable there are also a number of operators which combine arithmetic and bitwise operations with the assignment. The comparison operators determine equality or inequality and also the relative ordering of two numeric values — the comparison operation yields a **boolean** result. Logical operators include 'and', 'or' and 'not' — logical expressions appear in various Java programming constructs to control the flow of program execution. Bitwise expressions allow integer quantities to be manipulated at the level of individual bits — a common application is to use each bit as a flag to signal some condition. Java works with the `Unicode` character set — each character is an unsigned 16-bit quantity. A sequence of characters forms a string — a string constant should be enclosed in double quotes and the + operator may be used as a string concatenation operator. Each string is usually represented by a `String` object (often created implicitly) although other representations such as a **char** array are also possible. Simple input and output is achieved by calling functions of the `in` and `out` stream objects — these streams are typically connected to the keyboard and screen. The `in` and `out` streams are opened automatically and made available to the program as fields of the `System` class.

3. Statements

The Java language provides only a few program statement types and related keywords — however, nesting of statements one within another is permitted so that the basic elements can be combined to implement quite complex algorithms. This chapter summarizes the various statement types (simple, block and structured) which are available in Java. Program execution usually flows from one statement to the next in top-to-bottom order — however, some types of statement (transfer and structured statements) are designed specifically to modify this pattern of execution and these form the main topic of the chapter. The structured statements provided by Java include the conditional `if`, `if-else` and `switch` statements and the looping `while`, `do-while` and `for` statements — the `break` and `continue` transfer statements are commonly used to modify the operation of the looping statements.

3.1 Java Statement Types

A Java program consists of a collection of class (and interface) definitions — every class contains declarations for its field variables and also specifies the processing performed by each of its functions as a sequence of program statements ordered from top to bottom. There are essentially three sorts of these statements:

1. Simple statements
2. Block statements
3. Structured statements

Examples of simple and block statements have appeared in previous chapters — this chapter is principally concerned with introducing the structured statements. Simple statements are always terminated by a semi-colon (`;`) and come in three flavours:

1. Declaration statements
2. Expression statements
3. Transfer statements

Declaration and expression statements were discussed at length in the previous chapter. Examples of such statements include:

```
int i,j;
double average;
average = (float)(i+j)/2;
```

Program execution usually flows from one statement to the next but this natural flow may be broken and control transferred elsewhere by the occurrence of a transfer statement. The `break` and `continue` transfer statements are used in conjunction with the structured statements presented in sections 3.3 and 3.4 — they are discussed in section 3.5. The `return` transfer statement is used to terminate the execution of a function — the operation of functions in Java is covered in chapter 4.

3.2 Block Statements

A block statement is simply a collection of other statements bracketed by a matching pair of braces { } and serves to group the enclosed statements as a single statement. Note that no semi-colon appears at the end of a block statement:

{ Statement Statement ... Statement Statement }

A block statement is used where the syntax of Java permits only one statement but several statements are required to perform the necessary processing — in particular, each function must be defined by a single block statement. Of course, the statements enclosed by a block can themselves be block statements and so blocks can be nested to any depth. A variable whose declaration statement appears within a function block is local to the innermost block containing the declaration — the variable cannot be used outside this block. Furthermore, it is illegal to declare another local variable with the same name within any block contained by the first block.

For example:

```
public class Test {
  float x;

  public void print() {
    int x;
    {
      byte x; // illegal declaration
    }
  }
}
```

The first declaration of x occurs outside any function definitions and so defines a field of the Test class — chapter 5 covers classes in more detail. It is permissible for fields and local variables to use the same name — the latter is referred to as x but the former must be identified by the name **this**.x whenever confusion is possible. Note that the two variable types need not be related in any way. However, the third declaration of x is illegal and causes a compilation error — nonethess, if the second declaration is placed in its own inner block the problem disappears. A similar restriction applies to function parameters — in this respect parameters are treated like local variables defined at the top of the function block. For example:

```
import java.io.*;

public class Application {
  static float x = 3.142F;

  public static void main(String[] params) {
    int x = 3;
    System.out.println("local x = " + x);
    System.out.println("field x = " +
                                    Application.x);
  }
}
```

This program will print:

```
local x = 3
field x = 3.142
```

Here the simple name `x` refers to the **`int`** variable declared within the function block whilst the `Application` class name must qualify the name of the field — as explained more fully in the next chapter, the class name replaces the **`this`** keyword whenever static fields are referenced because such fields belong to the class as a whole rather than to individual objects. Without the local variable declaration the field can be referred to as `x` — this is the usual situation and hiding field names is not generally recommended.

The Java language supports multi-threaded applications. A 'thread' is a single sequence of program execution steps — with multiple threads a program can perform several different processing activities simultaneously. The topic of threads is covered in more detail by chapter 11 — however, note here that it is possible to coordinate the interaction between threads through the use of synchronized block statements. An ordinary block statement can be converted to a synchronized block statement by prefixing it with the keyword **`synchronized`** followed by an object specified in brackets:

```
synchronized (object) {
  // statements in block
}
```

At most one thread can be executing a block statement synchronized on any particular object — other threads synchronizing on the same object must wait until the currently active thread exits its block.

3.3 Conditional Structured Statements

Structured statements control how each thread of execution flows through a Java program. The syntax for a structured statement is defined by the Java language —

such a statement always contains one or more other statements within itself. There are two sorts of structured statement (discussed respectively in this section and the next):

1. Conditional statements
2. Looping statements

The simplest conditional statement is the **`if`** statement — this structured statement executes a contained statement conditionally according to the result of a logical expression.

> **`if`** (Expression)
>   Statement

The contained statement is executed if the bracketed expression is `true` — however, if the expression is `false` then control passes directly to the statement following the **`if`** statement and the contained statement is not executed. For example:

```
int count = 6;
if (count < 9)
  count++;
System.out.println(count);
```

The comparision `count<9` is `true` so the `count` variable is incremented and the value `7` is printed. There is also an **`if-else`** conditional structured statement:

> **`if`** (Expression)
>   Statement1
> **`else`**
>   Statement2

Here either Statement1 or Statement2 is executed (but not both) depending on whether the expression evaluates to `true` or `false`. The action is very similar to the `?:` operator described in section 2.6. For example:

```
if (x < 0)
  y = -x;
else
  y = x;
```

An equivalent statement involving the `?:` operator is:

```
y = (x<0) ? -x : x;
```

In both cases the `y` variable is made to hold the magnitude of `x` by reversing the sign of negative values.

As with block statements nesting of structured statements is possible — in fact (with a few restrictions) all statement types are interchangeable as far as nesting is concerned. An example of nested **`if-else`** statements follows:

```
System.out.print("The letter is");
if (letter == 'a')
  System.out.println(" 'a'.");
else if (letter == 'b')
  System.out.println(" 'b'.");
else
  System.out.println(" not 'a' or 'b'.");
```

The Java language provides the **`switch`** statement as an alternative method of coding such tests:

```
switch (Expression)
  BlockStatement
```

The above example may be recoded as:

```
System.out.print("The letter is");
switch (letter) {
  case 'a':
    System.out.println(" 'a'.");
    break;
  case 'b':
    System.out.println(" 'b'.");
    break;
  default:
    System.out.println(" not 'a' or 'b'.");
    break;
}
```

The **`case`** labels specify possible values of the bracketed expression which follows the `switch` keyword — the expression can be of any integer type except `long` (i.e. `byte`, `short`, `int` or `char`). Control passes to the statement immediately after the appropriate `case` label (or after the `default` label if no other labels match). The `break` statements transfer control out of the block contained by the `switch` statement — section 3.5 discusses transfer statements in more detail.

3.4 Looping Structured Statements

The second kind of structured statements are looping constructs — these repeatedly execute a series of program statements according to the value of a `boolean` expression. The simplest is the `while` statement which has the following syntax:

```
while (Expression)
    Statement
```

The processing performed by the `while` statement is depicted in the following figure.

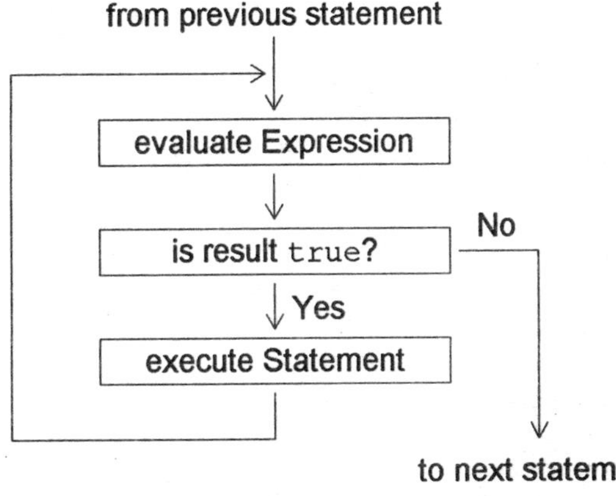

The contained statement forms the body of a loop which is repeatedly executed until the logical expression evaluates as `false` — the controlling expression must be of `boolean`

type. A typical application is to process the individual characters within a data stream one after another until the end-of-stream value is encountered — for example:

```
FileInputStream in =
  new FileInputStream("data_file");
int data = 0;
while ((data=in.read()) != -1) {
  // process character
}
in.close();
```

Here the `in` stream takes its data from a file — the `read()` function is called to retrieve the sequence of characters contained by the file. The **`while`** loop terminates whenever the `read()` function returns the value `-1` to indicate that the end of the file has been reached. Chapter 12 discusses the whole subject of input/output using Java in much more detail.

A slight variation of the **`while`** statement is the **`do-while`** statement which always executes the loop body at least once.

```
do
  Statement
while (Expression);
```

The operation of a **`do-while`** loop is depicted below.

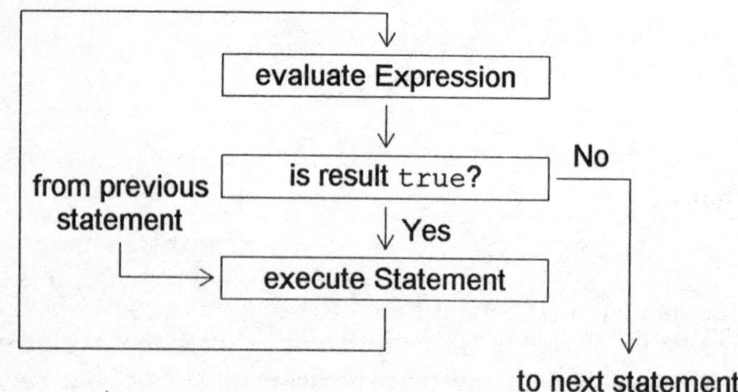

An example of using the **do-while** loop is provided by the conversion of an integer value to binary representation:

```
int i = 42;
System.out.print(i + " in binary is ");
StringBuffer s = new StringBuffer();
do {
  s.append(i%2==0?'0':'1');
  i /= 2;
} while (i != 0);
s.reverse();
System.out.println(s);
```

A `StringBuffer` object is needed here because the character sequence represented by a `String` object cannot be changed — the `append()` function adds characters at the end of the string held by the `StringBuffer` object and the `reverse()` function reverses the order of characters in this string.

The **while** loop (or the **do-while** variant) is typically used when the number of iterations is unknown beforehand — if, however, the number of iterations can be predicted then a **for** loop may be more suitable. The syntax of a **for** statement is as follows:

for `(`Initializer`;`ControlExpression`;`IterationExpressionList`)`
  Statement

In comparison to the **while** or **do-while** loop, the main difference is that initialization may be performed before the loop begins and after each pass through the loop an iteration expression list is evaluated — as with the **while** and **do-while** loops the control expression must yield a **boolean** result.

The **for** statement performs the processing shown in the following figure:

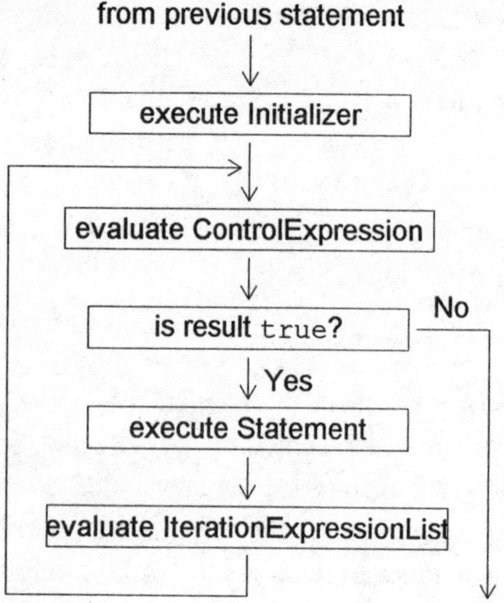

The initialization can either be an expression list or a variable declaration — any variables declared here exist only whilst the **for** loop is executing. The expression lists for initialization and iteration parts can include two or more expressions if they are separated by commas — the iteration expression list typically updates the value of a loop counter. For example:

```
int sum = 0;
for (int i=1; i<=100; i++)
  sum += i;
System.out.println("The sum is " + sum);
```

Here the first hundred integers are summed to calculate the value of `sum` and this value (`5050`) is then printed out.

3.5 Transfer Statements

The transfer statements include the **break**, **continue** and **return** statements. In general these statements transfer control out of some block statement which contains them — in particular, the **return** statement terminates execution of the block statement that defines a function. The **break** and **continue** transfer statements may appear within the block statement which forms the body of a loop (**while**, **do-while** or **for**) and so alter the usual flow of execution for the loop. The **break** statement immediately exits the loop — the **continue** statement ends the current iteration of the loop body and transfers control to the evaluation of the iteration expression list (**for** loop) or the controlling expression (**while** and **do-while** loops). Furthermore (as noted in section 3.3) the **break** statement may be used to exit from the block statement of a **switch** statement.

The **break** and **continue** transfer statements may also include a label following the keyword — the label must appear before some statement containing the transfer statement. For example:

```
start: {
        .
        .
    break start;
        .
        .
}
```

When the **break** statement is executed control passes out of the labelled statement to the following statement. For the **break** statement the labelled statement can be of any type — however, for the **continue** statement the labelled statement must be a loop (**while**, **do-while** or **for**) and the loop is not exited but instead the next iteration begins (after evaluating the iteration and control expressions as appropriate). The labels for statements can use the same names as local variables, function parameters, fields and functions, classes, interfaces and packages — however, such usage can be confusing. The `break` statement involving a label is about as close as Java comes to a `goto` statement — nonetheless `goto` is a reserved word in Java.

3.6 Trunk Calls

The following program illustrates some of the ideas from this chapter — the program gives the user three chances to guess the number of elephants in a telephone box.

```
import java.io.*;

public class Application {
 public static void main(String[] params)
           throws IOException {
  int elephants = (int)(10*Math.random());
  System.out.println("How many elephants?");
  DataInputStream data =
   new DataInputStream(System.in);
  int guess = 0;
  for (int i=1; i<=3; i++) {
   guess=Integer.parseInt(data.readLine());
   if (guess == elephants) {
    System.out.println("That's right !!!");
    break;
   }
   else if (guess > elephants)
    System.out.print("Too many!");
   else
    System.out.print("More than that!");
   if (i < 3)
    System.out.print(" .. try again ..");
   System.out.println();
  }
  if (guess != elephants)
    System.out.println("There are " +
             elephants + " elephants.");
  }
 }
```

The `random()` function from the `Math` class generates a

random number between `0.0` and `1.0` — this is used to determine the number of elephants making the trunk call. The **`break`** statement exits the **`for`** loop if the number of elephants is guessed correctly.

3.7 Summary

A Java program consists mainly of a sequence of class definitions — every class defines fields to hold its data and a collection of functions to process this data. The processing performed by a function is specified as a list of program statements which are, in general, executed in order from top to bottom. Statements come in three basic flavours — there are simple statements, block statements and structured statements. Simple statements may be declarations, expressions or transfer statements — the transfer statements (**`break`**, **`continue`** and **`return`**) terminate execution of an enclosing statement (or the current iteration of a loop). The structured statements are similarly used to alter the normal flow of control from one statement to the next — they execute a contained statement zero, one or more times depending on the value of an expression. There are conditional structured statements (**`if`**, **`if-else`** and **`switch`**) and looping structured statements (**`while`**, **`do-while`** and **`for`**) — a conditional statement selects one processing option from several whilst a looping statement repeatedly performs the same processing steps. Finally, it is possible to coordinate the activities of several concurrently executing threads by using a synchronized block statement.

4. Functions

All data processing in a Java program is performed by functions — the operating system initially passes control to the `main()` function and program statements within `main()` may invoke other functions. A Java function is a block of code which accepts a number of data items as input, performs various operations using these parameters and finally yields a result. Whilst the function is executing it may also produce side-effects such as opening a file, clearing the screen or updating a database. This chapter details the process of defining and invoking a Java function. A function definition specifies the function parameter list and return type — it also lists the processing steps which will be performed when the function is invoked. The chapter also discusses the function call semantics (call-by-value or call-by-reference) which are applied when actual arguments are passed to the parameters of a function. Finally, Java allows a function name to be overloaded by providing different implementations of a function corresponding to parameter lists of different types — the overloaded functions all share a common function name.

4.1 Java Functions

Chapter 1 outlined the use of functions in Java to perform data processing — in particular, whenever a Java program is run control passes to the `main()` function of a specified class. The `main()` function can invoke other functions and these in turn may call yet more functions — in fact, the total activity of the program stems from the execution of the `main()` function. Each Java function is a modular piece of code which accepts a number of data parameters, performs calculations using these parameters and finally generates a result — the result can be processed further within an expression statement. Every function must be defined within a Java class — the function belongs to the class and is often referred to as a 'method' of the class. The fields and functions belonging to a class can have the same names as each other — a function can always be recognized by the presence of an argument list. The functions specify the functionality provided by the class and they are generally designed to manipulate the data fields in a controlled manner. For example:

```
class Data {
  private int data;

  void data(int i) {
    data = i;
  }

  int data() {
    return data;
  }
}
```

Here the `data` field holds a piece of integer data. As explained more fully in the next chapter, the **`private`** keyword prevents code outside the class from directly manipulating the `data` field — instead the two `data()` functions are provided to store and retrieve data. To invoke the `data()` functions the following code may be executed:

```
Data panic = new Data();
panic.data(999);
int i = panic.data();
```

The first call to the `data()` function stores the value `999` in the `data` field of the `panic` object whilst the second call retrieves this value and places it in the `i` variable — the next section details the processing which occurs whenever a function is invoked. Using several functions with the same name is called 'function overloading' and this technique is discussed in section 4.3 — a common alternative here is to use the prefixes `set` and `get` to create the two distinct function names `setData()` and `getData()`.

The first `data()` function defined by the `Data` class accepts one parameter of type **`int`** and returns no result whilst the second function requires no parameters but returns a result of type **int** — the parameters appear in brackets following the function name whilst the return type precedes the name. If a function accepts two or more parameters they are listed one after another within the brackets and separated by commas — a function which requires no parameters is declared using an empty pair of brackets. If a function returns no result its return type is specified as **void** — otherwise the function should contain a **return** statement that provides the result returned by the function. Note also that a function which returns no value can terminate simply by reaching the end of the function block — an alternative is to terminate the function with a **return** statement, for example:

```
void data(int i) {
  data = i;
  return;
}
```

This usage is more common whenever the **return** statement occurs in the middle of the block statement.

The processing performed by a function is defined by a series of program statements enclosed by a matching pair of braces { } — in other words a function is defined using a single block statement. The general syntax for the full function definition is:

```
ReturnType FunctionName(ParameterList)
  BlockStatement
```

The function definition can also be preceded by a number of modifiers as illustrated by the `main()` function:

```
public class Application {
  public static void main(String[] params) {
        .
        .
  }
}
```

In particular, the **static** keyword means that the function belongs to the `Application` class as a whole rather than to individual objects of this class. Hence the `main()` function may be invoked as `Application.main()` without specifying an object. This should be contrasted with the `data()` functions of the `Data` class which do not use the **`static`** modifier — these functions require the existence of a `Data` object so that they can be invoked using an expression such as `panic.data()`. The distinction between class and object functions is discussed further in the next chapter. The **`public`** keyword attached to both the `Application` class and its `main()` function allows Java code outside the current package to invoke the `main()` function — such a function may be imported by files in other packages through the use of an **`import`** declaration. Chapter 10 deals in detail with Java packages but the following figure illustrates the basic idea:

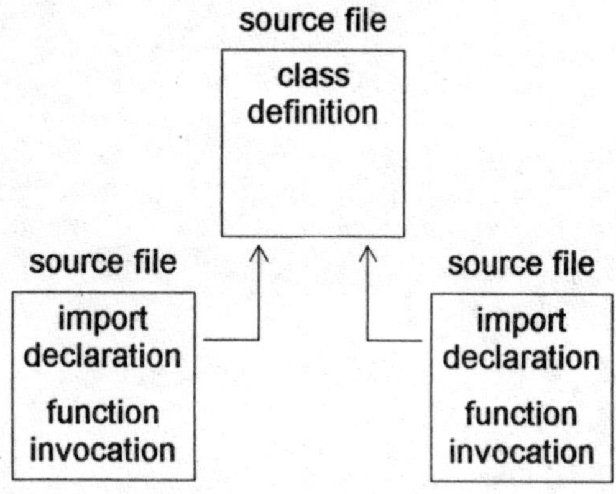

The function definition provides an implementation of the function by specifying a series of program statements within the function block. On the other hand, the function parameter list and the function return type define a communications interface between the function and any other code which wishes to invoke it. This approach of separating implementation from interface is the basis of object oriented programming — the next chapter discusses this important idea further. In particular, it is possible to specify a function's interface without providing any implementation of the function. Such a function is known as an 'abstract function' and the function modifier keyword **abstract** must prefix the declaration of the function — furthermore, the block statement usually needed to define a function is replaced by a semi-colon whenever the function is abstract.

Another keyword which acts as a function modifier is the **synchronized** keyword. A synchronized function acts as though its defining block statement were a synchronized statement as defined in section 3.2 — in this case the synchronization object is the one executing the function. The use of multiple threads with synchronized blocks and functions is described more fully in chapter 11.

4.2 Invoking a Function

This section examines the processing which occurs when a function is invoked. For each function invocation the parameters of the function are assigned actual values (arguments) — these are provided by the statement which invokes the function. The previous section showed two ways of invoking a function from a statement outside the class where the function is defined (namely by prefixing the function name with an object or with a class name) — to invoke a function from within the defining class just the simple name of the function can be used. For example:

```
class Alphabet {
  char letter = getLetter(13);
    .
    .
  char getLetter(int i) {
    .
    .
  }
}
```

Here the argument `13` is assigned to the `i` parameter which is entirely local to the block statement defining the getLetter() function. In particular, if the getLetter() function is invoked with a variable as an argument then i is initialized using the value of the variable — however, if i is subsequently modified these changes will not be reflected by the argument variable. For example:

```
int position = 13;
char letter = getLetter(position);
    .
    .
char getLetter(int i) {
  String alphabet =
    new String("abcdefghijklmnoqrstuvwxyz");
  return alphabet.charAt(--i);
}
```

Here the value of the position argument is copied to i during initialization of the parameter. Then i is decremented to account for the fact that character positions within a string are zero-based — however, the position variable itself is unaffected by the function call.

These semantics are known as 'call-by-value' since only the value of the argument is passed to the function — for intrinsic data types defined by the Java language (such as **int**) all parameter values are passed using call-by-value semantics. Similarly 'return-by-value' semantics are applied when returning the result of a function and the return type is an intrinsic Java type. For the getLetter() function the character selected from the alphabet string is copied to a temporary character variable and the function then returns the copy. The value of the temporary variable is available within the statement that invoked the function and so can be assigned to the letter variable. However, once the invoking statement finishes its processing the temporary variable disappears.

On the other hand, an object used as a function parameter is always passed to the function using 'call-by-reference' semantics. This means that a function can directly modify any object which it receives as a parameter — the function is not dealing with a copy of the object. Similarly, when a function returns an object result it uses 'return-by-reference' semantics — the actual object is returned and not a copy. In particular, if a function creates a new object itself and then returns this object to the invoking statement, the object will continue to exist even after the function completes its execution. For example:

```
String getString() {
  return new String("Hello!");
}
        .
        .
String hello = getString();
System.out.println(hello);
```

Here the `getString()` function generates a string which can be used even when the function invocation has terminated.

As an example of the difference between intrinsic data types and objects the following two `square()` functions accept parameters of type **`int`** and of class `Data` respectively:

```
void square(int i) {
  i = i*i;
}

void square(Data x) {
  int i = x.data();
  x.data(i*i);
}
```

These functions can be invoked using the following code:

```
int i = 3;
square(i);
System.out.println("i = " + i);
Data x = new Data();
x.data(3);
square(x);
System.out.println("x = " + x.data());
```

In the first case only the local copy of `i` is changed whilst in the second the original object `x` is modified — hence the code prints out the following:

```
i = 3
x = 9
```

Actually all function parameters and return values are copies but for objects this involves object references rather than the objects themselves — the next chapter discusses object references in more detail. Consequently the following code will not alter the original `x` object:

```
Data x = new Data();
x.data(3);
y = square(x);
System.out.println("x = " + x.data());
System.out.println("y = " + y.data());
    .
    .
Data square(Data x) {
  int i = x.data();
  x = new Data();
  x.data(i*i);
  return x;
}
```

The **new** statement in the `square()` function ends the connection between the parameter `x` and the original `Data` object — a new `Data` object is created, modified and eventually returned as the `y` object. Hence the code prints the following:

```
x = 3
y = 9
```

Finally, if a function has several parameters then they are evaluated in order from left to right. This fact may be important if the evaluation process has any side-effects.

For example:

```
int i = 1;
i = add(i++,i);
System.out.println("i = " + i);
    .
    .
int add(int i,int j) {
  return i+j;
}
```

Here the parameters i and j receive the values 1 and 2 respectively — the println() function displays the following message:

```
i = 3
```

It is impossible for the i and j parameters to be assigned in the opposite order thus causing the add() function to yield the value 2.

4.3 Function Overloading

An interesting feature of Java is its ability to support several functions all with the same name but having different types of parameters — this is known as 'function overloading'. The particular function invoked is determined by the types of arguments passed to the function. The actual selection procedure is quite involved but in essence each function invocation selects the best possible match from a set of functions which will accept the given parameters. However, the type of the function return value is not considered by the selection process so it is illegal for two functions to differ only in their return type. Furthermore, a **byte**, **short** or **char** parameter will not accept a constant integer argument even if the value is small enough to fit in the variable. Nonetheless, overloaded functions are generally easy to use — for example, the String class provides two versions of the substring() function:

```
public String substring(int start);
public String substring(int start,int stop);
```

The substring() functions are used to select a portion of a string — the first function takes all characters from the start position up to the end of the string whilst the second function just takes characters between the start (inclusive) and stop (exclusive) positions. A typical use of these functions is illustrated by the following code:

```
String hippo = new String("Hippopotamus");
System.out.print(hippo.substring(0,2));
System.out.print(" it's ");
System.out.print(hippo.substring(10));
System.out.println("!");
```

The first call to the substring() function invokes the version with two parameters and the second call invokes the version with one parameter — the code prints the following greeting:

```
Hi it's us!
```

Another example of function overloading is provided by the print() and println() functions of the PrintStream class — these accept a variety of parameter types including String and most of the intrinsic types. For example:

```
int i = 1;
boolean okay = (i < 2);
System.out.print("It is ");
System.out.print(okay);
System.out.print(" that ");
System.out.print(i);
System.out.println(" < 2");
```

Here three different versions of the print() function are called for String, **boolean** and **int** arguments — the following output is produced:

```
It is true that 1 < 2
```

The selection procedure for overloaded functions is applied at compile time. A further selection process involving overridden non-static functions may be applied at run time

— a detailed discussion of this complication appears in chapter 8.

4.4 Summary

This chapter has described the definition and invocation of Java functions. A function definition specifies the parameters accepted by the function, the processing performed using these parameters and the type of result returned by the function. A function may be invoked using the function name with a list of arguments being passed to initialize the function parameters — the result returned by the function can be further processed by the invoking statement. There are several ways to invoke a function — within the defining class the simple name may be used but outside this class the name should be prefixed by the class name or by an expression yielding an object (depending whether the function is static or not). A function may use the same name as a field belonging to the same class — furthermore, several functions in the same class can overload one function name provided they accept different parameter lists. Function parameters and return values are transferred using call-by-value and return-by-value semantics whenever intrinsic Java types are involved — however, for objects Java applies call-by-reference and return-by-reference semantics instead. In particular, this means that a function can modify any objects which it receives as parameters but for variables of intrinsic type the function works only with a copy and does not alter the original variable. The `return` transfer statement is used to terminate execution of a function — for a function with a return type other than `void` the `return` statement provides the value to return as the result of the function.

5. Classes and Interfaces

Java classes and interfaces form the basis for all object oriented mechanisms supported by the language. A class definition specifies the fields and functions which the class requires to implement the functionality that it provides — an interface definition is similar but contains only constant fields and abstract functions that are devoid of any implementation. Objects of a Java class are created using the `new` keyword which provides a reference to each newly created object. Thereafter external program code uses an object reference to send requests to the referenced object by invoking various functions — the object processes its own internal data fields and may acknowledge requests with replies supplied as the return values of the function invocations. The . (dot) operator is used to associate a function call with a particular object. The implementation details of an object are hidden from the outside world and all communications pass through the object's interface — this interface is specified by the parameter lists and return types of the functions defined by the object's class. In particular, the object's interface includes all functions declared by any Java interfaces which its class supports. A Java interface contains no code — its sole purpose is to force any class supporting it to implement a well-defined set of functions.

5.1 Java Classes

The standard Java class `Date` class allows a particular date (year, month and day) to be represented as a `Date` object — to illustrate how Java classes work this section looks at the implementation of a simplified version:

```
public class Date {
  private int year, month, day;
  public void setYear(int year);
  public void setMonth(int month);
  public void setDay(int day);
  public int getYear();
  public int getMonth();
  public int getDay();
}
```

A class specification such as this is often used to describe the fields and functions belonging to a class in a concise form — a class specification is not valid Java code because it does not provide any definitions for the processing performed by the class functions. As with most classes, the `Date` class defines a series of internal data fields and also provides a collection of functions to manipulate these fields in a controlled manner — the fields are declared using the **`private`** keyword and so can only be used directly by the `Date` class functions. Together the fields and the function definitions constitute the implementation of the `Date` class. On the other hand, the functions are declared as **`public`** and so form the interface provided by the `Date` class — section 5.3 further discusses the important notions of interface and implementation. The `year` field holds the year as a value relative to the year `1900`, the `month` field contains a value between `0` (January) and `11` (December), and the `day` field is set to the appropriate day (`1` to `31`) of the month. The three functions `setYear()`, `setMonth()` and `setDay()` store values in the corresponding fields whilst the `getYear()`, `getMonth()` and `getDay()` functions retrieve the stored values. The standard Java `Date` class uses the function names `setDate()` and `getDate()` in place of `setDay()` and `getDay()` — it also provides a `getDay()` function which returns the day of the week coded as a value from `0` to `6`. The next step in implementing the simplified `Date` class is to provide function definitions — the `set` functions are as follows:

```
public void setYear(int year) {
    this.year = year;
}

public void setMonth(int month) {
    this.month = month;
}

public void setDay(int day) {
    this.day = day;
}
```

Similarly the `get` functions have the following definitions:

```
public int getYear() {
  return year;
}

public int getMonth() {
  return month;
}

public int getDay() {
  return day;
}
```

The definitions illustrate several interesting points. Firstly (as noted in section 3.2) the parameters or local variables of a function can have the same names as class fields — here the names `year`, `month` and `day` are used for both fields and function parameters. Secondly, whenever the class fields are hidden in this way it is nevertheless possible to refer to the fields in other ways — for static fields the name must be prefixed by the class name (followed by the dot operator) whilst for non-static fields the keyword **`this`** is used as a prefix instead. As discussed in chapter 7 this latter usage is particularly common with constructor functions. Finally, in the `getYear()`, `getMonth()` and `getDay()` functions the fields are not hidden and so can be referred to by their simple names.

Fields and functions in the same class can have identical names — however, parameters and local variables within a single function cannot use the same names as one another. Also the relative ordering of fields and functions in a class definition is unimportant (except during initialization) — for example, in the `Date` class the `setYear()` function refers to the `year` field but the function definition can either precede or follow the field declaration.

Finally, a class can incorporate two essentially different types of fields and functions — there are fields and functions which belong to the class as a whole (static members) and there are fields and functions which belong to individual objects (non-static or 'instance' members). Static members are denoted by preceding them with the **static** keyword in the class definition — some utility classes such as the standard Java `Math` class contain only static members and so do not need to generate objects:

```
public final class Math {
    public final static double PI;

    public static double cos(double x);
    public static double sin(double x);
    public static double tan(double x);
        .
        .
}
```

A class contains a single copy of each static field but a new variable is generated for each non-static field whenever a new object is created. Similarly only the non-static functions are associated with individual objects — as explained in section 1.2 objects actually share the code for all of the functions defined by their class but non-static functions can use the **this** keyword to obtain a reference to the current object. The following section deals with non-static functions in more detail. Within the class definition the simple names of fields and functions will generally suffice — however, for code outside the class definition the situation is more complicated. A static member can be manipulated without reference to a particular object by prefixing the member name with the class name followed by the dot operator — the non-static members require an expression yielding an object instead of a class name. Using an object expression with a static member is equivalent to specifying the name of the class associated with the expression as determined at compile time — nevertheless, at run time the expression is evaluated and the object it yields is discarded.

The following example of using static members involves the `Math` class:

```
double pi = Math.PI;
double one = Math.tan(pi/4);
System.out.println("tan(pi/4) = " + one);
```

This code prints out the following message:

```
tan(pi/4) = 1
```

The next section concentrates more on the non-static members of a class.

5.2 Objects and References

Now that the `Date` class has been defined it is possible to create objects of the class — the creation of a new Java object usually involves the **new** operator. For example:

```
Date yesterday = new Date();
```

This statement actually performs three actions:

1. The `yesterday` variable is declared
2. A new `Date` object is created
3. A reference to the new object is assigned to the `yesterday` variable

In particular, the `yesterday` variable is not a `Date` object but rather holds a reference to a `Date` object — a Java program never manipulates objects directly but works with object references instead. It is possible to declare an object reference without also creating an object:

```
Date yesterday;
```

For a field the reference is initialized to the default value `null` — local variables declared within a function must be explicitly set before they are used. A reference variable can be associated with an object either by creating a new object or by copying a reference for an existing object from another variable — for example:

```
yesterday = new Date();
Date tomorrow = yesterday;
```

Here the `yesterday` variable is associated with a newly created `Date` object and then the `tomorrow` variable is declared and set to refer to the same object. If a reference variable holding a value other than `null` is assigned a new value then any association with the previously referenced object is lost — for example, after execution of the following statement the `yesterday` and `tomorrow` variables will reference distinct objects:

```
tomorrow = new Date();
```

Finally, if a null reference is displayed as a string then it is represented by the character sequence `"null"` — for example:

```
Date never = null;
System.out.println(never + " and void");
```

The fields of a `Date` object can be set using the `setYear()`, `setMonth()` and `setDay()` functions as follows:

```
yesterday.setYear(70);
yesterday.setMonth(0);
yesterday.setDay(1);
```

These function calls initialize the `yesterday` object so that it represents the date `1st January 1970` — chapter 7 describes a better way of initializing an object to a well-defined state using constructor functions. The field values can subsequently be retrieved with the `getYear()`, `getMonth()` and `getDay()` functions — for example:

```
int year = yesterday.getYear();
```

Every `Date` object contains its own personal copies of the non-static fields `year`, `month` and `day` defined by the `Date` class — consequently the non-static `Date` class functions perform different processing when executed by different objects. This fact is made explicit by the definition of the three `set` functions — for example:

```
public void setYear(int year) {
  this.year = year;
}
```

Here the **`this`** keyword provides a reference to the object currently executing the function — the **`this`** keyword cannot be used in static functions since they are not associated with any particular object. The keyword is needed in the `setYear()` function to differentiate the field from the parameter with the same name — this usage is particularly common in constructor functions. By contrast the three `get` functions do not use the **`this`** keyword explicitly but it is still applied implicitly — the functions consequently return the values held in the fields of the currently executing object.

An alternative way to describe the action of invoking a non-static function is to say that an object receives a message, performs some internal processing and sends back a reply if appropriate.

5.3 Interfaces

The technique of communicating with an object using messages allows the functionality of the object to be split into two:

1. Interface
2. Implementation

The communications interface fixes the format of messages sent and received by the object — it is specified by the function declarations appearing within the class definition in the form of parameter lists and return types. Upon receipt of a message, the object performs some internal processing — the implementation details are determined by the data structures which the object contains and by the function definitions for the class. The important point is that when the implementation is isolated from the interface then the internal workings of the object may be hidden from the outside world — this idea is known as 'encapsulation' and it is depicted in the following figure:

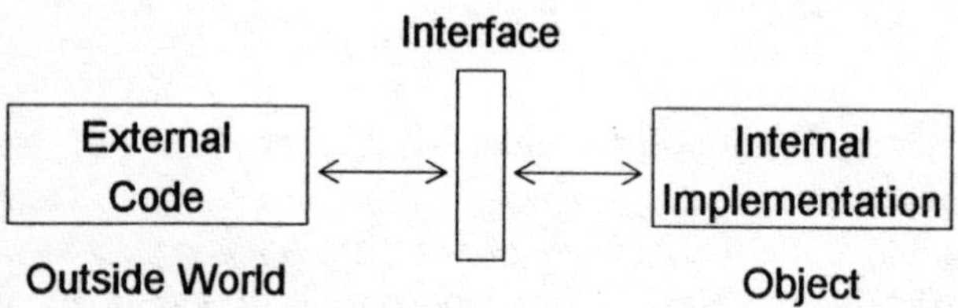

External code can continue to successfully communicate through the interface even if the implementation is changed. For example, the `Date` class previously described may change its implementation but retain the same interface:

```
public class Date {
  private long seconds;
  public void setYear(int year);
  public void setMonth(int month);
  public void setDay(int day);
  public int getYear();
  public int getMonth();
  public int getDay();
}
```

Here the date is stored internally as the number of seconds since `1st January 1970` — the standard Java `Date` class actually represents a date and time to the nearest millisecond. Existing external code will still function as before and need not be recompiled — indeed as long as certain rules for binary compatibility are observed Java is in general quite tolerant of modifications to interdependent classes where a full recompilation of existing code is not performed.

The Java language provides a couple of ways of formalizing

the notion of an interface:

1. abstract functions
2. interface definitions

A class can declare one or more of its functions as being abstract by applyng the **abstract** keyword to the function — the class does not provide any definition of the processing performed by the function and replaces the defining block statement with a semi-colon. For example:

```
abstract class Fruit {
  abstract void draw();

  String getName() {
    return "a fruit";
  }
}
```

Here the `Fruit` class defines one abstract function `draw()` and one non-abstract function `getName()`. The **abstract** keyword is also applied to the class itself since any class containing an abstract function must be declared as abstract — it is impossible to create objects which belong to an abstract class. Indeed the only purpose of declaring an abstract function is to specify the interface supported by a class — for example, the `Fruit` class `draw()` function accepts no parameters and returns a **void** result. The `draw()` function is intended to draw a picture of an actual fruit but no implementation is possible for the generic `Fruit` class. Chapter 8 shows how specific fruit classes such as `Apple` and `Banana` can be derived from the `Fruit` class — the abstract function declaration ensures that objects from all these fruit classes support the same communications interface as far as the `draw()` function is concerned.

The logical extension of this idea is to make all functions in a class into abstract functions — indeed interface definitions are designed for exactly this purpose. An interface definition is similar to a class definition but a Java interface can contain only two member types:

1. public abstract functions
2. public static final fields

The fields provide constants associated with the interface — the `PI` field from the `Math` class is an example of a constant field. Note that the fields and functions defined by a Java interface possess the required characteristics implicitly and there is no need to apply the corresponding modifier keywords. However, to use an interface outside of its package it is necessary to explicitly declare the interface as public.

A Java interface is used to group together a related set of functions and hence it defines one facet of an object's functionality — it allows a collection of otherwise unrelated classes to support the same set of functions. As long as the functions in the interface remain the same the underlying object may be changed — any object which supports the same interface will suffice. Of course, for this to work it is necessary to define the processing expected of each interface function — the Java interface only fixes the function parameter lists and return types. It is the responsibility of the implementor of a new class supporting the interface to adhere to the functionality specification. The interchangeability of objects that results when a number of classes implement a common interface is a classic example of 'polymorphism' — objects of different classes are sent the same messages through the interface but they perform their own individual processing. Indeed it is possible to define a reference variable for a Java interface and this can hold references for objects from any class that supports the interface. For example, Java defines the standard `Runnable` interface:

```
public interface Runnable {
  void run();
}
```

This interface allows an object to be used in the creation of a new thread — each thread is capable of executing a sequence of program statements concurrently with all other active threads. A thread's `run()` function acts in a similar fashion to the program's `main()` function — the `main()` function is executed by the primary program thread whilst the various `run()` functions are executed by secondary threads. Chapter 11 covers multi-threaded programming techniques in much more detail. The `Runnable` interface may be supported by a class simply by providing an implementation of the `run()` function:

```
class Hello implements Runnable {
  public void run() {
    System.out.println("Hello!");
  }
}
```

The **`implements`** keyword is used to denote that a class intends to support a particular Java interface — if the class in fact fails to implement all of the functions defined by the interface then it contains abstract functions and so must be declared as an abstract class. Anyway, the following code is now possible:

```
Runnable x = new Hello();
x.run();
```

The `x` variable is able to hold a reference to the newly created `Hello` object because the `Hello` class implements the `Runnable` interface — here the `Hello` object's `run()` function is called directly but this is not typical.

Finally, a class may implement more than one Java interface just by providing all the necessary function definitions — the various interface names are listed after the **`implements`** keyword and separated by commas.

The following figure depicts an object with two distinct interfaces:

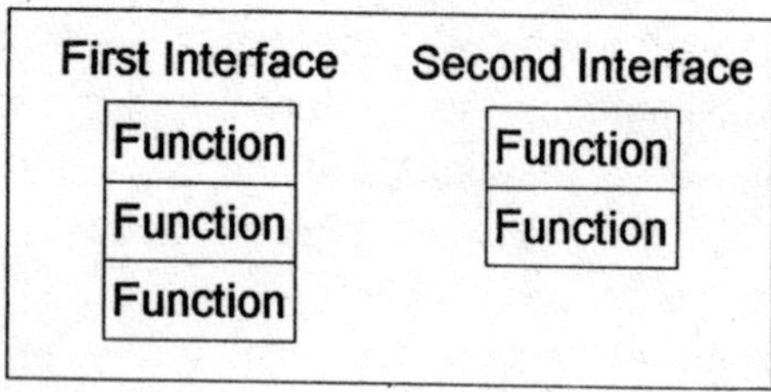

To permit one object to be substituted for another they must both support a common set of interfaces — the individual objects are polymorphic with respect to this shared set of interfaces. Of course, the two objects may also support other interfaces which they do not share but the polymorphism does not extend to these interfaces — furthermore, a class is free to define other functions besides those in the Java interfaces which it supports.

5.4 Notification Interfaces

Notification interfaces provide an interesting example of using Java interfaces. These interfaces are needed when an object wishes to notify the outside world of events that occur within the object — they complement other interface classes which permit messages to be sent to an object from the outside world. The following figure demonstrates the idea:

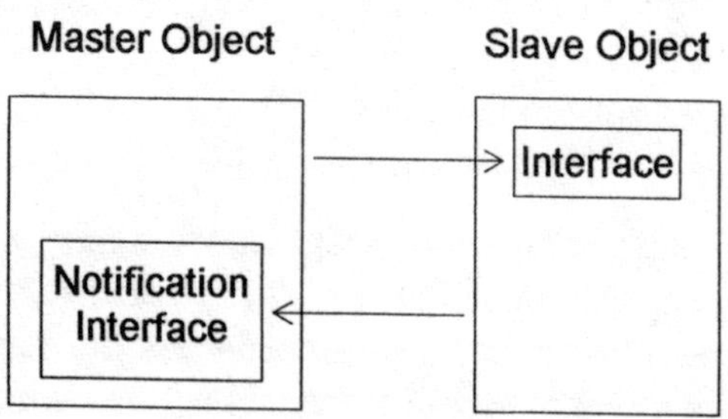

The `Master` object sends messages to the `Slave` object through the usual interface communications mechanism — if the slave wants to send messages back it passes them to a notification interface supplied by the master. The `Slave` class catalogues the sorts of messages it will send by defining an associated notification interface — for example, the notification interface `Notify` specifies two abstract functions:

```
interface Notify {
  int EVENT_1 = 1;
  int EVENT_2 = 2;

  void handleEvents(int event);
  void handleEvent();
}
```

This notification interface is designed to provide notification of three possible events that may occur within a `Slave` object — the function `handleEvents()` is called if either of the first two events occurs whilst the `handleEvent()` function is only called if the last event occurs. The function `handleEvents()` passes one of the constants `EVENT_1` or `EVENT_2` as a parameter to identify the relevant event.

Whenever a `Master` object wants to receive notifications from a `Slave` object it must implement the `Notify` interface. The `Master` class can implement the interface itself or it can define a helper class designed specifically for this purpose — the latter option is demonstrated here with the definition of the `Monitor` class. In particular, the `Monitor` class inherits the `EVENT_1` and `EVENT_2` constants associated with the `Notify` interface and so it can refer to them by their simple names — the constants do not need to be qualified with the `Notify` interface name.

The `Monitor` class has the following definition:

```
class Monitor implements Notify {
  public void handleEvents(int event) {
    if (event == EVENT_1) {
      // process first event
    }
    else if (event == EVENT_2) {
      // process second event
    }
  }

  public void handleEvent() {
    // process third event
  }
}
```

The `Slave` object must be able to send messages to its master's notification interface — a common technique is to pass an interface reference into the `Slave` class constructor:

```
class Slave {
  private Notify notify;

  Slave(Notify notify) {
    this.notify = notify;
  }
      .
      .
}
```

Now the `Master` object can create a `Slave` object and pass it a reference to the master's `Monitor` object:

```
Monitor monitor = new Monitor();
Slave slave = new Slave(monitor);
```

Since the `Monitor` class implements the `Notify` interface the reference is implicitly cast to `Notify` type. Now whenever an event occurs within the `Slave` object it can send a notification to the `Master` object — this is achieved with code similar to the following:

```
        .
        .
  if (notify != null)
    notify.handleEvents(Notify.EVENT_1);
        .
        .
  if (notify != null)
    notify.handleEvents(Notify.EVENT_2);
        .
        .
  if (notify != null)
    notify.handleEvent();
        .
        .
```

The `handleEvents()` and `handleEvent()` functions are invoked through a `Notify` interface reference but the code from the `Monitor` class is actually executed. The `Master` object thus receives notifications from its `Slave` object.

5.5 Garbage Collection

The **new** keyword is used to create new objects but there is no corresponding keyword to destroy objects when they are no longer needed — instead Java reclaims unused resources by the process of 'garbage collection'. The mechanism works by assigning each object a reference count — this is a count of the number of reference variables which are currently referencing the object. For example:

```
  yesterday = new Date();
  Date tomorrow = yesterday;
  tomorrow = new Date();
```

Here the first statement assigns a reference count of `1` to the newly created `Date` object — the second statement increases the reference count to `2` and the third statement reduces it back to `1` (whilst simultaneously setting the reference count for the new `Date` object to `1`). If the following statement is also executed then the reference count falls to zero:

```
yesterday = null;
```

For local reference variables like `yesterday` an assignment of `null` occurs implicitly whenever the function that contains them terminates — implicit assignments of `null` occur in other similar situations such as the destruction of an object containing fields that are reference variables. An object with a reference count of zero is no longer required by the program and so the resources it is consuming can subsequently be reclaimed by the garbage collector — as discussed in chapter 7 a class can define a `finalize()` function to assist in this endeavour. The Java Virtual Machine periodically runs the garbage collector in the background whilst the program is executing — the `gc()` function from the `System` class can be called to request that this action is carried out immediately.

5.6 Summary

A Java class can contain fields and functions — the fields hold data which may be manipulated in a controlled manner by calling the functions. In general, fields are either constant (denoted by the **`final`** keyword) or hidden from code outside the class (denoted by the **`private`** keyword). Functions are typically declared as **`public`** and form the interface provided by the class to expose its functionality to the outside world — a complex class may also define a number of internal helper functions to implement this functionality. The separation of interface and implementation is an important concept in object oriented programming — it allows objects to be interchangeable with one another. Java provides abstract functions and interface definitions to support the notion of an interface — the parameter lists and return types of the functions defined by a class (either directly or through Java interfaces) specify a communications interface between objects of the class and external code. Typically external code interacts with the object by invoking functions in its interface and receiving replies as return values. Notification interfaces are a complementary application of the Java interface mechanism — they allow an object to notify the outside world of internal events as soon as they occur rather than waiting passively for incoming requests. The members of a class (fields and functions) come in two basic varieties (static and non-static) — static members belong to the class as a whole whilst non-static members are associated with individual objects. In particular, whenever a new object is created it is allocated its own personal copies of all non-static fields defined by the class. Within a class its members are usually referred to by their simple names — however, the `this` keyword may be needed if a field is hidden by a local variable or function parameter (as is common in constructor functions). In code outside the class there are essentially three ways to refer to a class member all of which involve qualifying the member name with some prefix followed by the dot operator. The first alternative applies to static members and uses the class name as the prefix whilst the second alternative applies to non-static members and replaces the class name with an expression yielding an object — it is this object which will execute any function code and act as the object referenced by the `this` keyword. The third alternative combines an object expression with a static member — the compile time type of the expression determines the appropriate class name but the expression is still evaluated at run time and the result discarded. A new object can be created using the `new` keyword which also provides a reference to the new object. Indeed objects are always manipulated through references and the number of currently active references is maintained by Java as the object's reference count. Whenever the reference count drops to zero the object is no longer needed by the program and the memory storage allocated to it can be reclaimed — this is the job of Java's automatic garbage collector which runs periodically in the background during program execution.

6. Arrays

A Java class stores its data in a collection of fields that, in general, have a variety of different data types. Sometimes, however, it is necessary to process a set of items (such as a list of integers) that are all essentially identical — in such a situation Java arrays are especially valuable. Each array contains a series of elements that are distinguished only by an integer subscript value `0`, `1`, `2`, ... and so on. In particular, this arrangement allows an entire array to be processed within a Java looping structure (**`for`** or **`while`** statement) by selecting each element in turn with a loop variable. Every Java array supplies a `length` field that contains the number of elements held by the array — each time an array element is selected the subscript expression is checked to ensure that its value lies in the range between `0` (inclusive) and `length` (exclusive). This chapter describes how to create Java arrays (both single- and multi-dimensional) and how to manipulate the individual array elements — some common techniques for initializing and processing the data within an array are demonstrated. In particular, an array can be duplicated by invoking its `clone()` function.

6.1 Arrays

A Java class allows a collection of variables of different data types to be grouped together as the fields of an object — another possibility is to define an array of elements all of the same data type. The Java language provides built-in support for arrays in three ways:

1. reference variables for array types
2. use of the **`new`** keyword to create arrays
3. the subscript operator `[ ]` for selecting array elements

The creation of an array is in many respects similar to the creation of a Java object — indeed each array belongs to a class derived from the fundamental `Object` class as described in chapter 8. For example, the following statement creates an array with five elements of type **int**:

```
int[] x = new int[5];
```

As described in section 5.2 for objects, this statement actually performs the following three actions:

1. the reference variable `x` of type `int[]` is declared
2. a new array with five `int` elements is created
3. a reference to the newly created array is assigned to `x`

The individual elements may be referred to as to `x[0]`, `x[1]`, ... , `x[4]` — all arrays in Java are zero based. The elements of an array are initialized to zero for intrinsic types (`false` for **boolean**) and to `null` for reference types. It is also possible to set the initial values of the array elements explicitly with an array initializer list — for example:

```
int[] x = {7,8,6,9,5};
int total = x[0]+x[1]+x[2]+x[3]+x[4];
System.out.println(total);
```

Here the code uses an initializer list to set the array elements and then the individual values are summed — the next section discusses a much better way to process arrays by applying the Java looping constructs. The element values in an array are always mutable but the array reference can be declared using the **final** keyword if it is a field — in this case the field must be associated with an array during initialization and it continues to reference the same array throughout its existence.

The `x` array contains elements of an intrinsic Java type but it is also possible to create arrays that have objects as elements — for example:

```
Date[] january = new Date[31];
```

Here an array of `Date` reference variables is created and the individual elements are initialized to `null` — the elements must be assigned references to actual `Date` objects in subsequent program statements. An alternative approach is to provide the object references in an array initializer list as follows:

```
Date monday = new Date();
   .
   .
Date sunday = new Date();
Date[] week = {monday, ... ,sunday};
```

Furthermore, it is possible to declare an array for an abstract class or an interface. However, the elements of the array must belong to a non-abstract class which is derived from the abstract class or implements the interface — chapter 8 describes the process of deriving one class from another through the mechanism of inheritance. For example:

```
Runnable[] jobs = new Runnable[10];
```

Here the `jobs` array can hold references to objects from any class that implements the `Runnable` interface.

Finally, note that every array belongs to some Java class — the array class is determined by the element type of the array and the number of array dimensions. Each array class is created automatically by Java — the class of a particular array can be obtained using the `getClass()` function inherited from the `Object` class. For example:

```
boolean[] test = {true, false, false};
Class c = test.getClass();
System.out.println("array is from " + c);
```

Here the `toString()` function of the `Class` object is invoked implicitly to print the array class name as follows:

```
array is from class [Z
```

The lone `[` symbol denotes a single-dimensional array and the letter `Z` is a code for the **boolean** type — arrays with other element types have different code letters.

6.2 Arrays in Action

An individual element of an array can be selected using the `[ ]` subscript operator. An integer expression appears between the square brackets of this operator to specify the array element required — this expression can be of any integer type (**byte**, **short**, **int** or **char**) except **long**. The first element in an array has subscript 0, the next element has subscript 1 and so on — for example:

```
int[] x = {7,8,6,9,5};
int total = 0;
for (int i=0; i<5; i++)
  total += x[i];
System.out.println(total);
```

This code demonstrates how well arrays and the Java looping constructs (**for** and **while**) work together when processing a collection of similar items. Here is another more substantial example:

```
public class Application {
  public static void main(String[] params) {
    int size = params.length;
    int[] x = new int[size];
    int i,j,k,n;
    for (n=0; n<size; n++) {
      k = Integer.parseInt(params[n]);
      for (i=0; i<n && k>x[i]; i++);
      for (j=n; j>i; j--)
        x[j] = x[j-1];
      x[i] = k;
    }
    System.out.print("Sorted list:");
    if (size == 0)
      System.out.print(" empty");
    for (n=0; n<size; n++)
      System.out.print(" " + x[n]);
    System.out.println();
  }
}
```

This code performs an 'insertion sort' on an array of integers passed as command line arguments. An insertion sort is a simple method of sorting a list of items — starting with an empty list, each item in turn is inserted at the correct place in the list and any existing items at the end of the list are moved along to make room for the new item. Here the correct insertion position is determined by a **for** loop with a null statement as its body:

```
for (i=0; i<n && k>x[i]; i++);
```

The existing items in the list which follow the new item are moved by another **for** statement:

```
for (j=n; j>i; j--)
  x[j] = x[j-1];
```

Note in particular that every array automatically provides a count of the number of elements which it contains in a final field called `length` — this value is used here to create an `x` array of exactly the right size.

In addition to the `length` field every array also provides a `clone()` function that will create a copy of the array — the return value from the function is a reference to the new array and it should be cast to the appropriate array type. For example:

```
int[] x = {7,8,6,9,5};
int[] y = (int[])x.clone();
```

Here the complete `x` array is copied to the `y` array — an alternative approach is to use the `System` class `arraycopy()` function which allows a portion of the array to be selected for copying.

The array `clone()` function only performs a 'shallow copy' operation — this means that if the copied array contains reference values then only the references are duplicated and not the underlying objects or arrays. The essential idea is illustrated by the following figure:

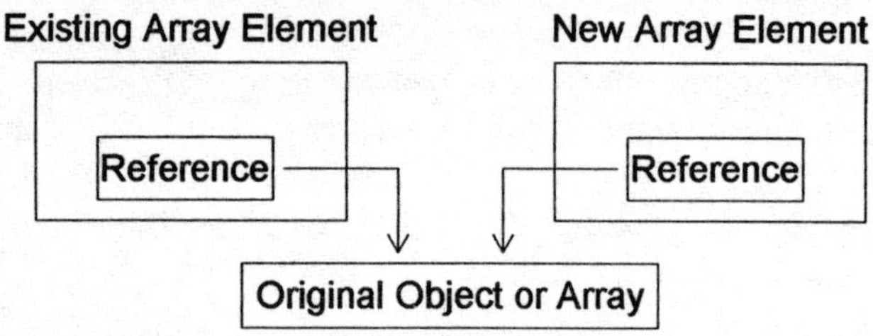

The topic of arrays containing arrays (multi-dimensional arrays) is covered in section 6.4.

6.3 Array Exceptions

There are a number of errors involving arrays which can occur at run time — Java reports these errors using exceptions as described in chapter 9. The occurrence of an exception will abruptly terminate execution unless the program is explicitly designed to handle the error.

During the creation of an array the system may be unable to supply sufficient storage space to accommodate the new array — in this case the error is reported with an `OutOfMemoryError` exception. Similarly, if an array dimension is specified as a negative value then Java generates an `ArrayNegativeSizeException` error.

When selecting an element from an array, the array reference and the subscript expression are fully evaluated first — the following errors may then be reported:

1. `NullPointerException` — the array reference is null
2. `ArrayIndexOutOfBoundsException` — the subscript is out of range

For an assignment to an array element these exceptions can occur either before or after the expression on the right-hand side of the operator is evaluated — for simple assignments the evaluation occurs first whilst for a combined assignment operation the exception preempts the evaluation. The assignment statement may eventually generate an ArrayStoreException error if the expression yields an object for storing that belongs to a class which is incompatible with the array type — chapter 8 provides an example of this situation.

6.4 Multi-Dimensional Arrays

The Java language supports multi-dimensional arrays by allowing arrays to be nested within arrays — several subscripts are needed to identify a fundamental element within the array. For example, a checker board may be represented as a two-dimensional array with one subscript for the row and another for the column. The declaration of a multi-dimensional array is quite straightforward:

```
int[][] board = new int[8][8];
```

The top left-hand square of the board would correspond to the element board[0][0] whilst for the bottom right-hand square the corresponding element would be board[7][7]. More generally, a square located by the values of row and column variables corresponds to the array element board[row][column]. As with function parameters (see section 4.2) the subscripts for a multi-dimensional array are fully evaluated one at a time from left to right — for example, the following code sets the array element board[1][2] to the value 3:

```
int i = 1;
board[i++][i] = 3;
```

No Java implementation will select the element board[1][1] instead.

The array declaration statement for the board array firstly creates an array of eight elements each corresponding to a different row — then for every row an array of eight elements of type **int** is created and a reference to this sub-array is stored in the appropriate element of the original array. The following figure illustrates the internal layout of a 4-by-4 `grid` array:

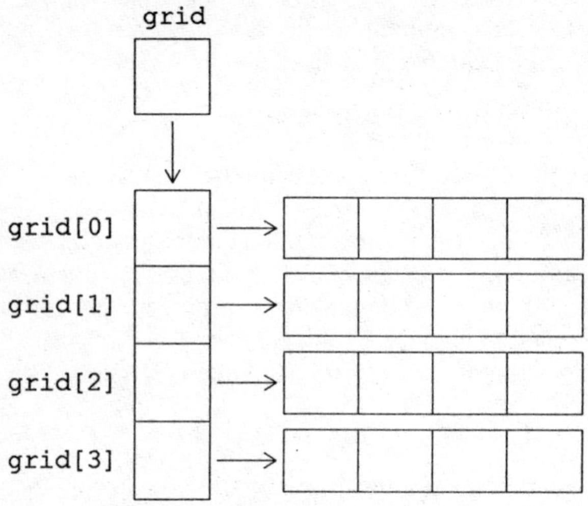

In fact the declaration for the `board` array is simply a short-hand notation for the following code:

```
int[][] board = new int[8][];
for (int i=0; i<8; i++)
  board[i] = new int[8];
```

In particular, it is possible to generate a Java array structure which is not rectangular — for example:

```
int[][] triangle = new int[8][];
for (int i=0; i<8; i++)
  triangle[i] = new int[i+1];
```

Here the `triangle` array structure contains only 36 integer elements instead of 64 — this technique can be useful in saving storage space when working with large (triangular) matrices in which the missing elements are all zero.

As for single-dimensional arrays the elements of a multi-dimensional array may be initialized using an initializer list — for example:

```
int[][] matrix = {{1,2},{3,4}};
int det = matrix[0][0]*matrix[1][1];
det -= matrix[1][0]*matrix[0][1];
System.out.println("determinant = " + det);
```

This code initializes a 2-by-2 matrix and then computes the determinant of the matrix.

6.5 Summary

A Java array is designed to hold a collection of identical items — these items can be simple data belonging to the intrinsic Java types or alternatively they can be references to objects or (in the case of multi-dimensional arrays) to sub-arrays. Each array belongs to a class derived from the fundamental Java class `Object` — in particular, this means that a new array is created with the **`new`** keyword and thereafter is manipulated through a reference variable much like an ordinary Java object. The individual elements from the array are selected using the `[ ]` subscript operator together with an integer expression that indicates the position of the required element within the array — for multi-dimensional arrays a number of subscripts are needed to specify a particular element. The elements of an array may be initialized to default values (zero, `false` or `null`) or they can be assigned particular values specified in an array initializer list. Arrays are well suited to processing a collection of similar items in a uniform manner. In this connection the Java looping strutures (**`for`** and **`while`**) work nicely with arrays — declaring an array to handle an abstract class or an interface is another useful technique. Every array provides a couple of standard members — the final field `length` holds a count of the number of elements contained by the array whilst the `clone()` function performs a shallow copy of the array and returns a reference to the newly created copy. Finally, there are a number of run time errors which are fairly common when manipulating a Java array — an `ArrayIndexOutOfBoundsException` error occurs when a subscript expression tries to select an element which is not contained within the bounds of the array and an `ArrayStoreException` error occurs when attempting to assign an object to an array of an incompatible type.

7. Initializers, Constructors and Finalizers

During the execution of a Java program many different classes may be needed and numerous Java objects can be created and destroyed. Before a particular class is used it must be loaded, linked and initialized by the Java Virtual Machine — thereafter objects can be created from the class. When an object is created, storage space is allocated to hold its own personal copies of any non-static fields defined by the class — deallocation of the storage occurs when the object is no longer referenced by the program. At creation the object may require initialization to place it in a well-defined state and to acquire any system resources that it utilizes — similarly during finalization the object can release any resources that it still holds before ceasing to exist. To define the initialization and finalization procedures for an object its class must provide constructor and finalizer functions — these are invoked implicitly by the Java Virtual Machine to perform the necessary processing. The constructor function may be overloaded to provide a variety of ways of initializing an object — Java supplies a default constructor if none are explicitly defined.

7.1 Class Initialization

The detailed process of combining a set of Java classes into a Java program is dependent on the particular Java implementation — however, the general procedure for introducing a new class involves the following three steps:

1. Loading
2. Linking
3. Initialization

The loading step ensures that the Java Virtual Machine has a copy of the byte code for the class and also that there is a `Class` object associated with the class. The linking step checks that the class code is valid, assigns storage space for the static fields of the class and sets these fields to default values (zero, `false` or `null`). Depending on the implementation Java may now resolve all references that the class makes to other classes — this approach typically involves a recursive application of steps 1 and 2 until all relevant classes have been loaded and linked. A common alternative is to postpone the resolution process until the other classes are actually needed. In any case, a class must be initialized (step 3) before it is used by the program — this step is designed to place the class in a well-defined state by initializing its static fields. This is the first time that any Java code defined by the class is executed — the loading and linking steps do not execute any class code. There are two ways to initialize the static fields — the first possibility is to provide an initializer value as part of the field declaration and the second option is to use a static initializer block. For example:

```
class Exchange {
  static int maxLines = 10;
  static Line[] phoneLines;

  static {
    phoneLines = new Line[maxLines];
    for (int i=0; i<maxLines; i++)
      phoneLines[i] = new Line();
  }
        .
        .
}
```

Here the `Exchange` class manages a set of ten phone lines in the static array field `phoneLines`. The declaration of the `maxLines` field uses an initializer value to set the number of available lines. On the other hand, the `phoneLines` array is initialized in a static initializer block — this alternative is preferable to using an array initializer list as follows:

```
static Line[] phoneLines = {new Line(),
                            ... , new Line()};
```

In general, the static initializer block provides more power than is possible with initialization in a declaration statement

— the latter option should be reserved for straightforward initializations.

The are a couple of important points to note about class initializers (of either kind). The first point is that they may only use static fields and functions — non-static class members are not available unless an object is created from the class. Secondly, the class initialization code is executed from top to bottom — furthermore, it is illegal for an initializer to reference fields which appear in the class definition below the initializer (although forward references to static functions are permitted). For example, the declaration for the `maxLines` field in the `Exchange` class must appear before this field is used in the static initializer block. One exception to the top-to-bottom initialization rule applies to final static fields that are initialized with a compile time constant — for example:

```
public final class Math {
  public final static double
    PI = 3.14159265358979323846;
        .
        .
}
```

Here the final static field `PI` from the `Math` class is a true constant — such fields are always initialized first and never appear to have the standard Java default values.

7.2 Object Creation

Once a class has been initialized objects belonging to the class may be created. Each object contains its own personal copy of every non-static field declared by the class — when a new object is created the Java Virtual Machine first checks whether there is sufficient storage space to hold all these new variables. If all is well the storage for the non-static fields is allocated and the variables are initialized with default values (zero, `false` or `null`) — otherwise an `OutOfMemoryError` exception is generated. The object must now be initialized to a well-defined state — this process is analogous to the initialization of a class but is a little more complicated. Object initialization involves the invocation of a special class function called a 'constructor' — the constructor function is invoked implicitly as part of the object creation process. For example, the `Exchange` class from the previous section creates a number of `Line` objects:

```
for (int i=0; i<maxLines; i++)
  phoneLines[i] = new Line();
```

As each of these objects is created the constructor function `Line()` is invoked. This constructor is defined by the `Line` class — all constructors take their name from the class that defines them.

```
class Line {
  Line() {
    // configure phone line
  }
      .
      .
}
```

The constructor performs initialization of each new `Line` object — this action is intended to configure the phone line to some well-defined initial state. A constructor function never returns a result and so it does not specify a return type — on the other hand, a constructor may accept zero, one or more parameters in the same manner as any other function. For example, the `Line` class could be modified so that its constructor accepts a **`long`** parameter which specifies the telephone number of a particular phone line to configure:

```
class Line {
  Line(long number) {
    // configure phone line
  }
      .
      .
}
```

In this case the parameter value must be supplied whenever a new `Line` object is created:

```
Line phone = new Line(999);
```

In general, a constructor should be used to completely initialize an object — the constructor parameters supply the necessary information to perform this initialization. For example, the `Date` class from section 5.1 could define a constructor that sets the `year`, `month` and `day` fields immediately without having to rely on the `setYear()`, `setMonth()` and `setDay()` functions to perform this task:

```
public class Date {
  public Date(int year,int month,int day);
        .
        .
}
```

Indeed the standard Java `Date` class adopts this approach.

A new object's non-static fields are initialized just before the program statements contained within its constructor body are executed — actually the full construction procedure is slightly more complicated than this but a detailed discussion is delayed until section 7.4 and chapter 8. An initialization value for a non-static field may be specified in the variable declaration for the field. As for class initialization the non-static fields are initialized in top-to-bottom order and it is illegal for an initializer to refer to a non-static field which is declared later in the class definition — however, initializers for non-static fields can reference any static class member no matter where it appears in the class definition. It is also permitted for non-static field initializer expressions to include the keywords **`this`** and **`super`** — chapter 5 introduced the former keyword and chapter 8 discusses the latter.

7.3 The Default Constructor

If a Java class does not explicitly define a constructor then it is automatically provided with a 'default constructor'

— the default constructor requires no parameters and acquires the same protection level (public or package) as its class. For example, the default constructor for some public class `Test` acts as though it had the following explicit definition:

```
public class Test {
  public Test() {
    super();
  }
      .
      .
}
```

The function body of the default constructor consists solely of the `super()` call. As explained in the next chapter this results in the execution of a constructor from the 'superclass' — all Java classes (except `Object`) are derived from their superclass which by default is the `Object` class. The `Test` class is declared as public and so its default constructor is public too — this means that `Test` objects can be created by any code in the program. On the other hand, if the `public` keyword is omitted then only code within the current package will be able to create `Test` objects.

A default constructor is specifically not generated if a class explicitly defines a constructor — this fact can be used to limit which code can create objects of a particular class. In particular, a public class can allow only code in its own package to create its objects by defining one or more constructors none of which are public — similarly any class can restrict object creation to just the class definition by defining one or more private constructors.

7.4 Constructor Overloading

A class can define several constructors each with a different parameter list — this is an example of the function overloading technique discussed in section 4.3. The `Complex` class will serve as an example of constructor overloading. Each `Complex` object represents a complex number — just as real numbers correspond to points on a line so complex numbers correspond to points in a plane:

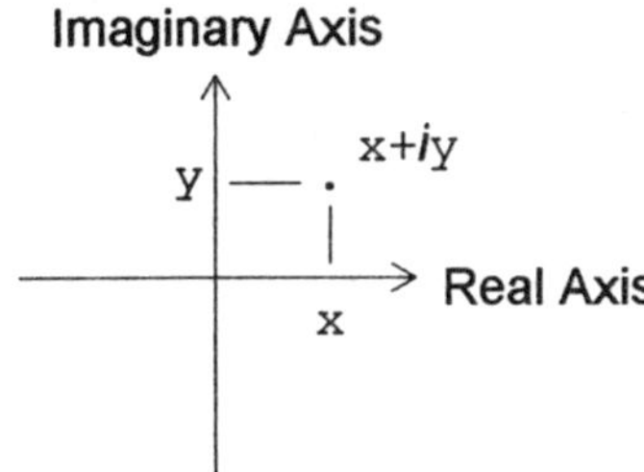

The point at coordinates (x,y) corresponds to the complex number x+*i*y — the x-axis is the real axis and the y-axis is the imaginary axis. The extraordinary thing about complex numbers is that *i***i* equals -1 but in other respects they act much like real numbers. The `Complex` class defines a pair of constructors:

```
class Complex {
  private double x;
  private double y;

  Complex(double x,double y) {
    this.x = x;
    this.y = y;
  }

  Complex(double x){
    this(x,0.0);
  }
        .
        .
}
```

The first constructor accepts two parameters and assigns them to the x (real) and y (imaginary) fields of the new `Complex` object. The second constructor is more interesting and is designed to convert a real number into a complex one by setting the imaginary part to zero — the second constructor calls the first using the keyword **this** rather than performing the necessary processing itself. This technique is common in Java and helps to avoid duplication of code — in general, the nested constructor call is followed by additional code that is specific to the calling constructor. For example, the `Complex` class could be redefined as follows:

```
class Complex {
  private double x;
  private double y = 0.0;

  Complex(double x,double y) {
    this(x);
    this.y = y;
  }

  Complex(double x) {
    this.x = x;
  }
        .
        .
}
```

The choice of constructor to invoke is made according to the usual rules for overloaded functions (see section 4.3) — for example:

```
Complex z = new Complex(1,1);
```

Here the first `Complex` class constructor is selected.

Do not confuse the two uses of the keyword **this** — when followed by the dot operator it references fields and functions and when followed by a parenthesized parameter list it performs a nested constructor invocation. Furthermore, the second usage is only valid as the first statement in a constructor function and the **this**`()` call is treated in a special way by Java. In particular, the initialization of non-static fields is delayed until the most deeply nested constructor call is reached — before initialization these fields have their default values. In the second definition of the `Complex` class the `y` field is only initialized just before execution of the statement:

```
this.x = x;
```

This is true no matter which of the two constructors is invoked initially. Incidentally, the explicit initialization of `y` is actually unnecessary here because it already has a default value of zero.

Since the **this**() constructor invocations appear as the first statement of another constructor it is often possible to assume that field initializations occur before execution of any constructor code. Indeed the details are only really important if Java inheritance is involved — chapter 8 provides a further discussion.

7.5 Finalization

As explained in section 5.5 Java relies on garbage collection to reclaim unused resources. The Java Virtual Machine is able to detect when an object is no longer needed by the program and to free the memory storage space allocated to the object. However, an object may be using other resources such as files, graphics or an external communications channel — to ensure that these resources are released in a controlled manner a class should define a finalizer function called `finalize()` which requires no parameters and returns a **void** result:

```
protected void finalize() {
  // release resources
}
```

The **protected** keyword is explained in the next chapter. Java calls the finalizer sometime after the object reference count reaches zero but before the object is finally discarded — the exact timing of these events is undefined but Java does guarantee to call an object's finalizer only once. The `finalize()` function should be regarded as the last line of defense against resource leaks — in normal operation an object will typically provide a function to explicitly control the release of resources. For example, the `Line` class from section 7.2 could define `connect()` and `disconnect()` functions to explicitly manage the state of a phone line:

```
class Line {
  private boolean connected;

  void connect() {
    connected = true;
  }

  void disconnect() {
    connected = false;
  }
      .
      .
}
```

The finalizer checks to see if the phone line has been properly disconnected — if it has not then the `finalize()` function must perform this action:

```
protected void finalize() {
  if (connected)
    disconnect();
}
```

Indeed all finalizers are typically programmed in this defensive manner.

In addition to the `finalize()` function a class may also define a `classFinalize()` function — whereas the former function is called whenever an object is destroyed, the latter is invoked when a class is unloaded

7.6 Life of an Object

To provide explicit initialization and finalization for an object its class must define constructor and finalizer functions — the constructor is implicitly invoked whenever the object is created and the finalizer is called whenever the object's reference count falls to zero.

For example:

```
class Test {
  Test() {
    System.out.println("Initializing ...");
  }
  protected void finalize() {
    System.out.println("Finalizing ...");
  }
}
```

The `Test` class performs no useful purpose except to demonstrate when the constructor and finalizer are invoked — the following program tests the `Test` class:

```
public class Application {
  public static void main(String[] params) {
    System.out.println("Before Creation");
    Test test = new Test();
    System.out.println("Object Exists");
    test = null;
    System.out.println("Reference Lost");
    System.gc();
    System.out.println("After Destruction");
  }
}
```

The program produces the following output:

```
Before Creation
Initializing ...
Object Exists
Reference Lost
Finalizing ...
After Destruction
```

The constructor is implicitly invoked to perform initialization when the `Test` object is created with the **new** keyword — the assignment of `null` to the `test` reference variable indicates that the `Test` object is no longer needed by the program and its finalizer should be executed. The call to the `gc()` (garbage collection) encourages the Java Virtual

Machine to finalize the `Test` object if this has not already happened automatically — nevertheless, it may be necessary to create and discard many `Test` objects before actually observing the `finalize()` function in action.

7.6 Summary

The Java Virtual Machine constructs an executing Java program by combining a collection of Java classes. Each class must be loaded and linked before it can be used — this process can be delayed until the class is actually needed. A class is initialized by allocating storage space for its static fields and setting these to default values — initializers in declaration statements and static initializer blocks are then executed in top-to-bottom order. A new object is created with its own personal copies of all non-static fields defined by its class — these are set to default values as the storage space is allocated. An object is initialized by invoking a constructor function — any non-static fields declared with initializer expressions are initialized before the constructor code is executed. A class may define several different contructors provided they each accept distinct parameter lists — the choice of constructor follows the usual rules for selecting an overloaded function. Java will provide a default constructor for any class that does not define one explicitly — the default constructor accepts no parameters and simply invokes the superclass constructor taking no parameters. A default constructor is specifically not provided if a class defines at least one constructor explicitly — this fact can be used to control the creation of objects from a particular class. Whenever an object is no longer referenced by the program, the storage space allocated to it is reclaimed by the Java Virtual Machine's garbage collector. A class may define a finalizer function to assist in releasing unused resources — Java runs the finalizer of an unreferenced object exactly once sometime before the object is discarded.

8. Inheritance

Inheritance is the principal mechanism in Java for implementing polymorphism — a collection of objects are polymorphic if they exhibit a range of different behaviours upon receipt of identical messages. Encapsulation and polymorphism form the foundations of the object oriented programming philosophy — encapsulation is concerned with hiding implementation details whilst polymorphism allows diverse functionality to be exposed to the outside world through a well-defined communications interface. All Java classes are ultimately derived from the `Object` class through a chain of other Java classes — consequently all Java objects are polymorphic with one another at some basic level. Each Java class in the inheritance chain derives many of its characteristics from its superclasses but it can modify or extend these as required. In particular, each derived class inherits the communications interface defined by its superclass and any Java interfaces that it supports — when different function implementations are provided by different derived classes a range of polymorphic objects is made available. This chapter covers several topics that relate to Java inheritance including the derivation of a new subclass from an existing superclass, the mechanisms for inheriting, hiding or overriding superclass fields and functions, the four protection levels provided by Java, and finally the initialization and finalization procedures for Java objects.

8.1 Superclasses and Subclasses

In Java every class (except `Object`) is derived from some other class called the 'superclass' of the derived class — the derived class is a 'subclass' of the other class. In general, a class may have many subclasses but it has exactly one superclass — the `Object` class has no superclass and acts as a default superclass for any class which does not explicitly specify its superclass. Hence each Java class is ultimately derived from the `Object` class through a chain of other classes — in particular, this derivation chain has only a single strand.

A subclass inherits many of its characteristics from its superclass — these fall into three categories:

1. Data
2. Code
3. Interfaces

The next few sections cover the inheritance of data and code whilst a discussion of Java interfaces is delayed until later in the chapter. In general, the data fields defined by a superclass are present in all objects of its subclasses — each subclass may add more data fields if it needs them. Similarly, the functions of the superclass are inherited by objects of the subclasses — an exception to this rule is that a subclass does not inherit any constructor functions defined by its superclass. Furthermore, the inheritance of class characteristics applies to static fields and functions — however, the static data fields for the superclass and the subclass are distinct. Section 8.3 describes how protection keywords can be used by a class to prevent any subclasses from inheriting particular fields and functions. Conversely, the keyword `final` can be applied to individual class members to force all subclasses to inherit them directly — the derived classes are not allowed to re-define final fields and functions.

The `final` keyword can prefix a class definition to prevent derivation from the class — otherwise any Java class can act as a superclass. Nonetheless, a good superclass is specifically designed as such — in particular, a superclass should ideally contain only functionality that is sufficiently general to make it widely applicable. Indeed Java supports inheritance principally to provide a mechanism for software reuse — the source code defined by a superclass need not be duplicated for each of its subclasses.

8.2 Deriving a Subclass

The derivation of a new Java class from a previouly existing one is straightforward. The following definition for the `Derived` class states that it inherits from the `Original` class:

```
class Derived extends Original {
      .
      .
}
```

The subclass name is followed by the **`extends`** keyword and then the superclass name. In general, the subclass can use its inherited fields and functions exactly as if it had defined them itself. As an example, suppose the `Original` class has a `data` field and also a `printData()` function:

```
class Original {
  int data;

  void printData() {
    System.out.println(data);
  }
}
```

The `Derived` class can create objects just like any other class:

```
Derived object = new Derived();
```

Such objects inherit their characteristics from the `Original` class — the inherited fields and functions can be treated as though the `Derived` class had defined them directly:

```
object.data = 0;
object.printData();
```

However, reference variables for the superclass can reference objects belonging to the subclass. Indeed, a subclass reference will be implicitly cast to a superclass reference when required — for example:

```
Derived derived = new Derived();
Original original = derived;
```

Here there is an implicit cast from `Derived` reference type to Original reference type before the original variable is assigned the reference to the Derived object. Casts in the opposite direction from superclass references to subclass references must be explicitly requested:

```
Derived derived = new Derived();
Original original = derived;
derived = (Derived)original;
```

Furthermore, casts between superclass and subclass references are the only type of reference casting permitted by Java — it is illegal to cast between reference types for two unrelated classes. The **instanceof** operator can be used to test if an object belongs to a particular class or one of its subclasses — the Java Virtual Machine will report a ClassCastException error if a program attempts a cast where the **instanceof** operator would yield a false result. For example:

```
void processObject(Original original) {
  if (original instanceof Derived) {
    Derived derived = (Derived)original;
    // process Derived object
  }
  else {
    // process Original object
  }
}
```

Here the original variable can reference an Original object or a Derived object — the **instanceof** operator is used to test whether the original reference can be cast to Derived type.

Finally, as noted in the previous section, the Derived class may itself act as a superclass for yet another derived class — the fields and functions defined directly by the Derived class as well as those inherited from the Original class are available to be inherited by a new subclass. In this way a chain of classes can be built with each class inheriting from the previous one in the chain — the Object class is found at the start of every such chain. For the classes in this section the derivation chain consists of the `Object`, `Original` and `Derived` classes.

8.3 Protection Keywords

The **`private`**, **`protected`** and **`public`** keywords guard against improper use of class fields and functions. The **`private`** and **`public`** keywords have appeared in many classes in previous chapters — the **`protected`** keyword is only relevant when inheritance is involved. The **`public`** keyword allows any source code to reference a field or a function — the **`private`** keyword prevents any code outside the class definition from referring to a particular class member. Furthermore, the private members of a class are not inherited by any of the subclasses derived from the class. In many instances where inheritance is involved, the **`private`** and **`public`** keywords provide protection control that is too coarse. A derived class may need fields or functions from the superclass — the **`private`** keyword is too restrictive but the **`public`** keyword releases all control. In these situations the **`protected`** keyword should be applied to the relevant fields and functions in the superclass definition — protected class members can be used by functions in any classes derived from the superclass.

There is a fourth level of protection (default) which fits between the private and protected protection levels — this applies whenever there is no protection keyword explicitly specified. Default protection restricts references to class members to the current package — furthermore, members with default protection are not inherited by derived classes defined outside the package. Chapter 10 provides more details on Java packages — however, note that since the protected protection level is less restrictive than the default protection level, class members defined with the **`protected`** keyword are in fact available to all classes in the current package.

Finally, Java requires that the protection applied to a

function (static or non-static) is not increased by the inheritance process — whenever a new subclass is derived the protection level for each function must stay the same or be modified from default to protected to public. However, this restriction does not apply to fields.

8.4 Field and Function Hiding

Derived classes may define new fields and functions in addition to those that they inherit from their superclass. For example:

```
class Original {
  protected int item;
        .
        .
}

class Derived extends Original {
  private float[] list = new float[100];
        .
        .
}
```

Here the superclass has the integer `item` field — this is inherited by the `Derived` class which also defines a new `list` field. If the same name is used for fields in both the superclass and the subclass then the latter field hides the former — within the functions of the derived class the name refers to the subclass field. Furthermore, the types of the superclass and subclass fields need not be related in any way — for example:

```
class Derived extends Original {
  private float item;

  void setItem(float data) {
    item = data;
  }
        .
        .
}
```

Here the `setItem()` function assigns a value to the floating-point field of the `Derived` class and not the integer field inherited from the `Original` class. Java provides the **super** keyword to permit the hidden field from the superclass to be referenced by the subclass — for example:

```
class Derived extends Original {
  private float item;

  void setItem(float item) {
    this.item = item;
  }
  void setItem(int item) {
    super.item = item;
  }
      .
      .
}
```

Here the `setItem()` function is overloaded to permit either superclass or subclass field to be set. The first `setItem()` function is modified to illustrate an explicit use of the **this** keyword introduced in chapter 5 — the previous definition of the `Derived` class applies the **this** keyword to the `item` field implicitly. The **super** keyword is similar to the **this** keyword but refers to the superclass instead of the class itself. In particular, the **super** keyword must be associated with an object and cannot be used during class initialization or within a static function — however, in these situations the name of the superclass may be substituted for the **super** keyword.

Static fields are inherited just like non-static fields. Furthermore, a static field can be hidden by a non-static field defined in a subclass and vice versa — however, the equivalent statement for functions is not true. A static function can only be hidden by another static function and a non-static function can only be overridden by another non-static function — the next section deals with function overriding. A static function is only hidden by a subclass function that has the same name and accepts parameters of the same types — other superclass functions having the same name but different parameter lists are not hidden but inherited. Finally, a hidden function must have the same return type as any function which hides it. As an example of function hiding the `Original` and `Derived` classes can be modified as follows:

```
class Original {
  private static int item;

  static void setItem(int data) {
    item = data;
  }
}

class Derived extends Original {
  private static int item;

  static {
    setItem(0);
    Original.setItem(0);
  }

  static void setItem(int data) {
    item = data;
  }
}
```

The static initializer block explicitly zeroes both the `item` fields — note that these fields have a default value of zero anyway. The first function call to `setItem()` invokes the `Derived` class function — the hidden superclass version must be invoked using the `Original` class name as a qualifier. An alternative method of invoking a hidden static function is to replace the superclass name with the **super** keyword — however, this is not possible during class initialization or within a static function.

8.5 Function Overriding

The previous section described the hiding of static functions — non-static functions behave somewhat differently to static functions with regards to inheritance. A non-static function defined in a subclass with the same name and parameter types as a superclass function overrides the superclass function rather than hiding it — as for function hiding the two non-static functions must have the same return type. As an example of function overriding the `Fruit` superclass may be defined as follows:

```
class Fruit {
  void whoAmI() {
    System.out.print("I am ");
    getName();
  }

  protected void getName() {
    System.out.println("a fruit.");
  }
}
```

The `whoAmI()` function is invoked to tell a `Fruit` object to print a description of itself whilst the `getName()` function actually supplies the name of the fruit. The `Fruit` class is specifically designed as a superclass that represents all kinds of fruit and so its `getName()` function is general. The following code:

```
Fruit fruit = new Fruit();
fruit.whoAmI();
```

prints the message:

```
I am a fruit.
```

Now that the `Fruit` superclass has been defined specific fruit classes can be derived from it — the derived classes will print a particular fruit name when the `whoAmI()` function is invoked. For example, the `Apple` fruit class is defined as follows:

```
class Apple extends Fruit {
  protected void getName() {
    System.out.println("an apple.");
  }
}
```

The `Apple` class inherits the `whoAmI()` function and overrides the `getName()` function. An `Apple` object may be created and the `whoAmI()` function invoked:

```
Apple apple = new Apple();
apple.whoAmI();
```

This executes the code for the `whoAmI()` code from the `Fruit` superclass — if the `getName()` function were static the result would be:

```
I am a fruit.
```

However, the following situation now arises:

1. A superclass function is executed by an object from a subclass
2. The superclass function invokes a non-static function
3. The object's subclass overrides the non-static function

In these circumstances the superclass function must call the subclass version of the non-static function.

Here the superclass function is `whoAmI()`, the object is `apple` and it belongs to the derived `Apple` class which overrides the non-static `getName()` function. Hence the `whoAmI()` function must use the `Apple` class version of the `getName()` function. The `apple.whoAmI()` call thus produces the message:

```
I am an apple.
```

When the `whoAmI()` function is invoked for objects of different classes (`Fruit` or `Apple`) the processing that is performed differs. This is an example of the fundamental object-oriented mechanism of polymorphism introduced in section 5.3 — the next section provides another example.

Finally, note that the **`super`** keyword also works with non-static functions — it allows an object to select a function defined in the object's superclass even if its own class overrides the function. However, this usage is only possible within the class definition — furthermore, the **super** keyword cannot be applied during class initialization or within a static function. In particular, attempting to invoke an overridden function from external code by using a cast on a reference variable will not work — this technique is only applicable to hidden fields and functions.

8.6 Reference Variables

The previous two sections have discussed the selection of a static or non-static function when the function invocation is made from within the class definition. Generally, these function calls can be made using the simple function name — for non-static functions this actually involves an implicit application of the **this** keyword. This section extends the ideas to cover function invocations made using a reference variable or expression. For static functions the decision as to whether to call the superclass function or an overriding version from a derived class is made at compile-time — for non-static functions the final decision is left until run time and the choice depends on the class of the referenced object.

For a static function invoked using a superclass reference variable the superclass version of the function is always used — this is true even if the variable references an object of some subclass that hides the superclass function. To provide an example the following modifications are made to the `Fruit` class:

```
class Fruit {
  static void whoAmI() {
    System.out.println("I am a fruit.");
  }
}
```

and to the derived `Apple` class:

```
class Apple extends Fruit {
  static void whoAmI() {
    System.out.println("I am an apple.");
  }
}
```

The code below demonstrates the choice of static function:

```
Fruit fruit = new Fruit();
Fruit apple = new Apple();
fruit.whoAmI();
apple.whoAmI();
```

Both calls to `whoAmI()` print the message:

```
I am a fruit.
```

To obtain the proper response from the `apple` object it is necessary to cast its reference variable to `Apple` type:

```
((Apple)apple).whoAmI();
```

Now the subclass function is invoked — in general, to obtain the subclass version of a static function, a subclass object must be referenced by a reference variable for the subclass.

The choice of non-static functions is not made at compile time but at run-time and the class of the referenced object is more important than the type of reference variable involved. For a superclass object the non-static function defined by the superclass is invoked — similarly for a subclass object referenced by a subclass variable, the subclass function is invoked. The interesting case occurs when:

1. A superclass variable references an object of a subclass
2. The reference is used to invoke a non-static function
3. The object's subclass overrides the non-static function

This situation exactly mirrors that involving the implicit **`this`** pointer as discussed in the previous section — consequently, the subclass version of the non-static function is invoked. As an example, the `Apple` and `Banana` classes are both derived from the `Fruit` superclass and this class is again modified by the removal of the **`static`** keyword from the `whoAmI()` function:

```
class Fruit {
  void whoAmI() {
    System.out.println("I am a fruit.");
  }
}

class Apple extends Fruit {
  void whoAmI() {
    System.out.println("I am an apple.");
  }
}

class Banana extends Fruit {
  void whoAmI() {
    System.out.println("I am a banana.");
  }
}
```

The following code processes an array of fruit objects:

```
Fruit[] basket = {new Apple(),new Banana()};
for (int i=0; i<basket.length; i++)
  basket[i].whoAmI();
```

When the `whoAmI()` function is called for each of the fruits in the basket, the appropriate derived class version of the non-static function is chosen — the code consequently prints the following:

```
I am an apple.
I am a banana.
```

This is another example of polymorphism — the `Apple` and `Banana` objects perform different processing when the `whoAmI()` function is invoked.

The `Fruit` class and its subclasses also introduce a few important points concerning arrays and inheritance. An array variable can be assigned a reference to an array whose element type is actually a subclass of the class specified in the declaration statement for the array variable — for example:

```
Fruit[] basket = new Apple[10];
```

Here Apple is a subclass of Fruit so the basket variable can be assigned a reference to an array of Apple objects. However, in a situation such as this it is possible to produce a run time error by attempting to store an object of an incompatible class in the array — the result is that Java reports an ArrayStoreException error. For example:

```
Fruit[] basket = new Fruit[10];
basket[3] = new Banana(); // okay
basket = new Apple[10];
basket[3] = new Banana(); // error
```

Here it is permitted to store a Banana object in a Fruit array but trying to store a Banana object in an Apple array generates a run time error.

All fields (both static and non-static) used by external code are selected at compile time according to the type of the reference — in particular, the overriding mechanism does not apply to non-static fields. In any case most fields are, in fact, hidden from external code — notable exceptions are constant fields such as PI from the Math class.

8.7 Constructors

The standard procedure for creating and destroying an object was discussed in chapter 7 — there are a number of other considerations when inheritance is involved. When a new object is created the Java Virtual Machine performs the following three steps:

1. Storage Allocation
2. Superclass Initialization
3. Subclass Initialization

The object is allocated sufficient storage to hold the non-static fields defined by its class and all other classes from which this class is derived — lack of storage space is reported by an `OutOfMemoryError` exception. The fields are all set with default values (zero, `false` or `null`) — initialization using the expressions from field declaration statements is performed later. The next stage in the object creation process involves a chain of constructor calls. The first action of every constructor (except the default `Object` class constructor) is to call another constructor either in the same class or in the superclass. These nested constructor calls are made using the **`this`** and **`super`** keywords followed by a parenthesized parameter list — the `Complex` class defined in section 7.4 provides an example. If no nested constructor call is explicitly specified then an implicit call is made to the superclass constructor with an empty parameter list. The constructor call chain ends when the default `Object` class constructor is reached — this constructor performs no processing but the non-static fields defined by the `Object` class are initialized at this time. The next class in the chain then initializes its non-static fields and runs its constructor — this process continues with all initialization for a particular class being completed before control is returned to its subclass. In particular, the fields defined by a subclass still have their default values whilst a superclass constructor is executing — this fact may be of interest because function overriding is possible during the construction process. For example:

```
class Original {
  Original() {
    display()
  }

  void display() {}
}

class Derived extends Original {
  int x = 1;

  void display() {
    System.out.println("x = " + x);
  }
}
```

The creation of a `Derived` object produces the following message:

```
x = 0
```

The subclass version of the `display()` function is invoked by the superclass constructor — at this time the `x` variable still has its default value of zero. As described in section 7.3 the `Derived` class is supplied with a default constructor of the form:

```
Derived() {
  super();
}
```

This is an example of the general rule that creation of a Java object always results in a call to a constructor for the object's superclass either explicitly or implicitly. On the other hand, if a class defines a finalizer function then the superclass finalizer is not automatically invoked — it is usually a good idea to call the superclass finalizer explicitly:

```
protected void finalize() throws Throwable {
  // finalization for subclass
  super.finalize();
}
```

Here the subclass performs its own finalization before invoking the superclass finalizer.

8.8 Interfaces

Java interfaces were introduced in section 5.3 — each Java interface definition specifies the parameter lists and return types for all the functions in that interface. In particular, although a class has only a single superclass it can implement many different Java interfaces. The class inherits its communications interface from its superclass and each of the Java interfaces that it implements — it is therefore possible for the class to inherit a number of different functions all with the same name and parameter types. This is illegal unless each of these functions also has the same return type — however, if the return types are identical then the class can provide a single function definition (or inherit one from its superclass) and this will implement all of the inherited abstract functions. The class also inherits all of the constant fields associated with its Java interfaces — if several fields with the same name are inherited they must be referred to using qualified names in order to avoid ambiguity. Finally, it is possible for one Java interface to be derived from another in much the same way as for Java classes — for example:

```
interface Original {
        .
        .
}

interface Derived extends Original {
        .
        .
}
```

However, for interfaces the **extends** clause can contain a comma-separated list of several super-interfaces — this is analogous to the **implements** clause for a class. All these possibilities mean that a class can inherit from a particular interface in several different ways — nevertheless, the class can reference any constant fields associated with such an interface using just their simple names and this is not considered to be ambiguous.

8.9 Summary

All Java classes are ultimately derived from the `Object` class through a chain of other Java classes — each class in the chain (except `Object`) inherits from exactly one superclass. The creation of a new object thus results in a chain of nested constructor calls leading back to the `Object` class — the first action of every constructor (except the default `Object` class constructor) is to invoke (implicitly or explicitly) another constructor from the same class or from the superclass. However, if a class defines a finalizer it must explicitly call the superclass `finalize()` function whenever this is required. The Java inheritance mechanism allows a class to treat fields and functions from its superclass in much the same way as members defined directly by the class. The protection levels private (most restrictive), default, protected and public (least restrictive) can be applied to control the inheritance process on a member-by-member basis. A class may also inherit from one or more Java interfaces by implementing the abstract functions defined by the interface — the class inherits the interface function specifications (parameter lists and return types) and any constants associated with the interface. Furthermore, a Java interface can inherit from one or more other interfaces — indeed this is the only mechanism provided by Java to support multiple inheritance. An inherited field (static or non-static) can be hidden by a similarly named field defined in a subclass — the types of the two fields need not be related in any way. An inherited function can be hidden or overridden by a subclass function with the same name and parameter types — the two functions must have the same return type. A static function may only be hidden by another static function and a non-static function may only be overridden by another non-static function. The **`final`** keyword prevents individual fields or functions from being re-defined in a derived class — alternatively it can be used to inhibit derivation from a particular class altogether. Fields and static functions are selected at compile time according to the type of the expression used to reference them — the **`super`** keyword, an explicit cast or a class name can be used to specify a superclass member. On the other hand, the final selection of a non-static function is delayed until run time and the choice depends on the class of the object that will execute the function — in this case the **`super`** keyword is the only way to specify that a superclass function should be invoked.

9. Exceptions

Java exceptions provide a mechanism for structured error handling. Whenever an error is detected an exception may be thrown — this action passes information about the error from the point in the program where the error occurs to a higher level handler that knows how to deal with the problem. The Java language defines the **`try`**, **`throw`**, **`catch`** and **`finally`** keywords to support its exception mechanism. Typically a section of code which may throw an exception is enclosed within a **`try`** block and thrown exceptions are caught by handlers that supply the error processing — in this way the program statements which perform the basic processing are separated from those which handle errors. Any exceptions which are thrown but not caught by a function are passed to the invoker of the function — the function declaration must include a list of these exceptions. The Java exception mechanism is fully integrated with rest of the Java language and the Java Virtual Machine throws an exception whenever it detects a problem with the program execution.

9.1 Error Handling Schemes

The traditional approach to error handling is not structured — there are typically three options on finding an error:

1. Generate an error code
2. Transfer the flow of control
3. Terminate the program

An error code may be returned as the result of a function or used to set an error variable. In either case the responsibility for handling the error is simply passed on — the error code should be tested at some point but this is not always done. For example, in the C language allocation of memory storage space is achieved by calling the `malloc()` function and this function returns a null value whenever there is insufficient free memory to satisfy the request — the returned value should always be checked to ensure that the new memory has actually been allocated but this rarely happens.

The second option upon encountering an error is to transfer control to a set of program statements that will process the error — an 'error handler'. This approach also requires constant checking for the occurrence of an error with the result that the main purpose of the code is often obscured. Other computer languages provide the `goto` statement for transferring program control in exceptional circumstances but this option is not available in Java — the nearest equivalent is the labelled `break` statement described in section 3.5. In any case this approach generally only allows control to be transferred within the current function and this may not be the best place for the error handler code.

Finally, it may be impossible to handle an error satisfactorily and the only remaining option is to terminate the program — the `System` class provides the `exit()` function to halt the Java Virtual Machine when serious errors occur. A slightly less drastic alternative is to terminate execution of an individual thread whenever it encounters a fatal error — chapter 11 discusses the operation of Java threads in more detail.

In many situations the processing of errors can be elegantly handled by the Java exception mechanism. The technique combines the 'error code' and 'control transfer' approaches by passing error information directly from the point at which the error occurs to the error handler. This has several advantages:

1. Once an error is detected it cannot be overlooked
2. Most code can assume there are no errors
3. The error and its handler may be widely separated

The first statement holds since control is always transferred when an error is detected — furthermore, control will only flow normally if no errors are encountered so the second statement follows. Finally, errors usually occur within low-level routines which do not understand the context of the error sufficiently well to be able to handle them — this job is much better suited to higer level routines but these rarely bother to check for error codes generated by the functions they invoke. The exception mechanism can transfer information about the error directly from a low-level routine to its high-level handler.

9.2 Java Exception Classes

A Java exception is an object belonging to some class derived from the standard Java class `Throwable` — the action of reporting an error using an exception is known as 'throwing an exception'. The `Throwable` class is a subclass of the `Object` class and also the superclass of two other standard Java classes (`Exception` and `Error`) — furthermore, the `RuntimeException` class is a subclass of the `Exception` class. This hierarchy of exception classes mirrors the way in which Java handles the various exceptions — section 9.5 describes how Java treats the subclasses of `Error` and `RuntimeException` in a special manner. The `Error` exceptions result from problems associated with the Java Virtual Machine and user-defined exception class should inherit from the `Exception` class — a program may attempt to handle exceptions belonging to subclasses of the `Exception` class but recovery from exceptions derived from the `Error` superclass is typically impossible. The subclasses of the `RuntimeException` class report many common run time errors such as using a null reference to refer to an object or attempting to manipulate an array element located beyond the bounds of the array.

Most of the interesting exceptions generated by Java belong to subclasses of the `RuntimeException` class. Indeed many of the `RuntimeException` classes have appeared in earlier chapters — for example, the `ClassCastException` exception is thrown whenever an incompatible cast is attempted and an `ArrayStoreException` error is generated if the program tries to assign an object of an incompatible type to an array element. Two other examples relating to arrays are ArrayNegativeSizeException and ArrayIndexOutOfBoundsException — these are thrown for bad subscript values supplied either when the array is created or when selecting an array element. Yet another example is the ArithmeticException error which is thrown if an integer divide-by-zero is attempted — dividing a floating-point quantity by zero just produces an infinite result. A NullPointerException error occurs if a program uses a null reference to manipulate a field or invoke a function — however, this rule does not apply to static members since these can be referenced by an expression yielding null without causing an error. Finally, the OutOfMemoryError exception is thrown whenever there is insufficient memory to create a new object or array — the OutOfMemoryError class is a subclass of Error rather than RuntimeException. When creating a new object the exception is thrown immediately, even before the evaluation of any constructor parameters — on the other hand, the dimensions for a new array are fully evaluated before an OutOfMemoryError condition is detected. Other notable exception classes not derived from the RuntimeException class include IOException and InterruptedException — the former exception is used if an input/output operation encounters an error whereas the latter is needed if a thread is interrupted whilst it is waiting for some event.

9.3 Exception Keywords

The Java language provides the **try**, **throw**, **catch** and **finally** keywords to support its exception mechanism. As noted in the previous section the process of reporting an error with an exception is known as 'throwing an exception' — the **throw** keyword is used to throw an exception:

```
throw new Exception("Whoops !!!");
```

Here the **throw** statement causes the error message "Whoops !!!" to be passed to an error handler — for

Java to find a suitable handler the code must be enclosed in a **try** block:

```
try {
      .
      .
  throw new Exception("Whoops !!!");
      .
      .
}
catch (Exception e) {
  System.out.println(e);
  System.exit(999);
}
```

The **try** block is followed by a **catch** block which contains the code for the error handler. In fact, any number of error handlers can follow a **try** block each with their own **catch** block — the different handlers are distinguished by the type of exception that they catch. The code within the **catch** blocks is only executed if an exception is thrown from the **try** block — if no exception is thrown then control passes directly to the statement following the last **catch** block. Similarly, if an exception handler is indeed invoked but it completes normally by reaching the bottom of its **catch** block then control again passes to the statement following the last **catch** block. Section 9.5 deals with the case where an exception is thrown but there is no suitable exception handler available. In any event a **finally** block can be placed after the list of **catch** blocks (or directly after the **try** block if no **catch** blocks are defined). The code in the **finally** block is executed no matter how the **try** block is exited — the **finally** block runs after the **try** block (and possibly a **catch** block) but before control is passed elsewhere in the program. The **finally** block is typically used to ensure that any resources allocated in the **try** block are correctly released — for example:

```
Socket s = null;
try {
  s = new Socket("andromeda",1234);
      .
      .
}
finally {
  if (s != null)
    s.close();
}
```

Here the **try** block opens an Internet socket connection to the host computer andromeda using the port number 1234 — the **finally** block ensures that the socket is properly closed. Chapter 14 deals with sockets and related low-level techniques for communicating over the Internet.

9.4 Throwing Exceptions

The following code provides an example of working with exceptions — in particular, it demonstrates how the code that performs the main processing is separated from the error handler.

```
int i,j,k;
DataInputStream data =
          new DataInputStream(System.in);
while (true) {
  try {
    System.out.println("First integer?");
    i = Integer.parseInt(data.readLine());
    System.out.println("Second integer?");
    j = Integer.parseInt(data.readLine());
    k = i/j;
    System.out.print(i + "/" + j);
    System.out.println(" = " + k);
  }
  catch (ArithmeticException e) {
    System.out.println("Divide by Zero");
  }
}
```

The **while** loop repeatedly asks for two integers and prints out the result of dividing one by the other — the code within the **try** block can be written under the assumption that division by zero will not occur. If the Java Virtual Machine does indeed detect an attempt to divide by zero it throws an exception of type ArithmeticException — the exception is caught by a handler and the following message is printed:

```
Divide by Zero
```

The **while** loop then continues to ask for another pair of integers. The important point to note is that the basic processing (input, division, ouput) can assume no errors will occur — the error handler is completely separate from the rest of the code.

The previous example uses a standard Java exception thrown by the Java Virtual Machine — the next example instead throws a user-defined exception explicitly using the **throw** keyword. The first step is to derive a new exception class from the Exception class:

```
class MathException extends Exception {
  MathException() {
    super();
  }

  MathException(String s) {
    super(s);
  }
}
```

An exception class typically provides two constructors — one constructor requires no parameters and the other accepts a String object that holds an error message. Here the constructors simply invoke the corresponding functions in the Exception superclass. The error message can be retrieved with the getMessage() function inherited from the Throwable class — alternatively the toString() function also supplies the exception class name. Of course, an exception class is free to define other constructors if it needs to supply an error handler with more information about the cause of an exception. In any case the previous example can now be recoded using the MathException class:

```
try {
    .
    .
 if (j == 0)
   throw new MathException("Divide by Zero");
 k = i/j;
 System.out.print(i + "/" + j);
 System.out.println(" = " + k);
}
catch (MathException e) {
 System.out.println(e.getMessage());
}
```

A final variant will demonstrate the selection of a suitable error handler when a **try** block has several catch blocks associated with it. The DivideByZeroException class is derived from the MathException class as follows:

```
class DivideByZeroException
              extends MathException {
  DivideByZeroException() {
    super("Divide by Zero");
  }

  DivideByZeroException(String s) {
    super(s);
  }
}
```

Now the **try-catch** code is modified so that it throws

a `DivideByZeroException` object:

```
try {
    .
    .
  if (j == 0)
    throw new DivideByZeroException();
  k = i/j;
  System.out.print(i + "/" + j);
  System.out.println(" = " + k);
}
catch (DivideByZeroException e) {
  // specific error processing
  System.out.println(e.getMessage());
}
catch (MathException e) {
  // general MathException processing
}
catch (Exception e) {
  // general error processing
}
```

The **catch** blocks following the **try** block are scanned from top to bottom until a suitable exception handler is found. The exception class specified in brackets after the **catch** keyword determines the range of exceptions that a particular handler can accommodate — exceptions from this class or any of its subclasses are acceptable. Here the `DivideByZeroException` exception is caught by the first catch handler — other types of `MathException` object would be passed along to the second handler and even more general `Exception` objects are caught by the third handler. The next section describes what happens whenever no suitable exception handler can be found in the list following the **try** block. Finally, each **catch** block also specifies a name for the exception that it catches — this name is entirely local to the **catch** block but it must not hide the name of a local variable or parameter defined in the function containing the **catch** block. Furthermore, any variables declared within the **catch** block must not be given the same name as the exception.

9.5 Unhandled Exceptions

If a handler cannot be found in the **catch** block list following a **try** block then the exception is passed on to any dynamically enclosing **try** block and the process repeats — the same thing happens if an exception is thrown from within a **catch** handler. In particular, if a function throws an exception and this exception is not caught within the function then the exception is passed along to the invoker of the function — to alert the invoking code that such an event may occur the function must list the exception class after the keyword **throws** in the function declaration. For example, the standard Java class `Thread` has a `sleep()` function that causes the current program execution thread to halt for a given number of milliseconds:

```
public static void sleep(long timeout)
        throws InterruptedException {
                    .
                    .
}
```

It is possible to awaken the thread from its slumber prematurely and this causes the `sleep()` function to throw an `InterruptedException` exception — this fact is indicated using the **throws** keyword and the exception class name. If a function may throw several different exception types these should appear as a comma-separated list following the **throws** keyword. Furthermore, if a function is hidden or overridden then the new version cannot extend the **throws** list but it can shorten it or alternatively replace a class with some subclass. In fact the **throws** list only need include 'checked exceptions' — this specifically excludes exceptions from subclasses of the `Error` and `RuntimeException` classes.

Whenever an exception has been thrown and the outermost **try** block is reached without a suitable handler being found, the current program thread will terminate. However, the thread first executes the function uncaughtException() provided by its ThreadGroup object — this prints a stack trace showing the exact point in the program where the exception occurred. The Throwable class defines the functions fillInStackTrace() and printStackTrace() for explicitly manipulating an exception's stack trace — typically the stack trace is filled in automatically whenever the exception is created.

9.6 Summary

The Java exception mechanism provides a way to handle errors in a structured manner — exceptions combine the traditional error handling techniques of generating an error code and of transferring program control to an error handler. A Java exception is an object from some subclass of the standard Throwable class — an error is reported by throwing an exception. This approach allows detailed information about an error to be passed directly from a low-level routine where the error occurs to a high-level routine that knows how to handle the problem. The exception mechanism is fully integrated with the rest of the Java language — Java defines many standard exception classes as subclasses of the Throwable, Exception, Error and RuntimeException classes. The Java language provides the **try**, **throw**, **catch** and **finally** keywords to support its exception mechanism. Any code which may throw an exception is typically enclosed within a **try** block and the associated error handlers are defined in **catch** blocks — a **finally** block may be used to provide code that must be executed no matter how the **try** block is exited. A **catch** handler specifies the class of exception which it can accept — exceptions from any subclasses will also be processed. If no suitable handler can be found then the exception is passed along to any dynamically enclosing **try** block — this process may be repeated until the outermost **try** block is reached. As a last resort the current thread calls the uncaughtException() function to print a diagnostic stack trace and then terminates. If a function generates an exception that it does not itself catch, the exception class must be included in the function's **throws** list to alert any invoking code of this fact — however, this rule specifically does not apply to exception classes derived from the standard `Error` and `RuntimeException` classes.

10. Packages

The basic unit of a Java software distribution is the package — each package contains a collection of related class and interface definitions. Java classes from different packages may be combined together to form a complete program. The Java language itself defines a number of standard packages — the most important of these is the `java.lang` package and the Java types defined by this package are made available to all Java programs automatically. A new class or interface is placed in a particular package using a package declaration statement — similarly an import declaration statement can be used to import a single type or alternatively all types provided by a package. A package is able to control the availability of its classes and interfaces using the **`public`** keyword — references to individual class fields and functions can be further controlled by assigning them to the private, default, protected or public protection levels. This chapter describes the Java package mechanism and concludes with an example of how to code a new user-defined Java package.

10.1 Package Organization

A set of related Java classes and interfaces may be arranged into a package — only classes and interfaces defined using the **`public`** keyword are available to code outside the package. Each file in a package generally defines a single type (class or interface) and the filename is formed by combining the type name with the extension `.java` (or a similar extension) — the files for all classes and interfaces belonging to the package are typically placed in a directory named after the package. A file is assigned to a particular package by including a package declaration at the start of the file — for example:

```
package demo;
        .
        .
```

Here any class or interface contained in the file becomes

part of the `demo` package — to refer such types outside the `demo` package it is necessary to qualify the simple type name by prefixing it with the package name and the dot (`.`) operator. For example, if the `Application` class is defined in the `demo` package then `demo.Application` is its qualified name. A new Java type which is not explicitly placed in a package is assigned to the default package — this usage is designed only for small in-house programs.

In addition to classes and interfaces a package can also define sub-packages and these are assigned sub-directories of the package directory — files for classes or interfaces in each sub-package appear in the corresponding sub-directory. The package name can be used to qualify each of the sub-package names in much the same way as for classes and interfaces — in particular, fully qualified package names must be used in any package declaration statements. However, within the class and interface definitions of a package each of the sub-packages can be referred to by their simple names — note that a sub-package cannot have the same name as any class or interface defined by the package. The package hierarchy is principally designed to indicate the logical relation of one package to another — hence, in many respects, a sub-package must be treated like any other package. Java itself defines a number of standard packages that are all sub-packages of the `java` package:

`java.lang` — basic language features
`java.util` — assorted utility classes
`java.io` — input/output processing
`java.awt` — Abstract Window Toolkit
`java.applet` — Java applets
`java.net` — Internet communications

These packages are described in much more detail in the remaining chapters of the book.

Simple package names are acceptable for casual Java development where the packages will not be widely distributed. More generally a unique package name should be generated by reversing the components of an Internet domain name and adding final components to describe the individual project — the first component of the new package name (for example `COM` or `UK`) is capitalized.

10.2 Protection Keywords Revisited

Section 8.3 described the four levels of protection (private, default, protected and public) provided by Java for fields and functions — each class or interface is similarly assigned either public or default protection. A class or interface is only available outside its package if it is declared using the **`public`** keyword — otherwise it has default protection and is available just throughout its package. The protection afforded to the individual fields and functions in a visible class further restricts the availability of the various members. The **`private`** keyword prohibits references to a particular field or function in any code appearing outside the class definition — similarly, the default protection level prevents references in code located outside the package. The protected protection level is slightly more relaxed than the default level and also allows references by derived classes that are defined outside the package — in particular, a constructor function defined using the **`protected`** keyword can be invoked with a **`super`**`()` call from outside the package. Finally, the public protection level places no additional restrictions on the use of a field or function — in this case the protection level of the class or interface determines whether the member is available outside the package or not.

10.3 Importing Classes

If the Java implementation makes a particular package available to a program, then all public classes and interfaces in the package are available. However, the types must be referred to using qualified names consisting of the package name and the type name separated by a dot — an explicit import declaration is needed to allow code within one package to use a simple name to reference a type defined by a different package. However, the classes and interfaces defined by the standard package `java.lang` are automatically imported by every Java program and can always be referred to using simple names — the next chapter discusses the `java.lang` package in more detail. An import declaration must appear in every file where it is desired to import a particular type — import declarations are placed directly after the package declaration, and definitions for classes and interfaces follow the import declarations. There are in fact two kinds of import declaration statement:

1. import-single-type
2. import-on-demand

The first variety imports a single specific type. On the other hand, the second variety can import all the classes and interfaces from a particular package — however, only those types that are actually needed will be imported. In both cases the import declaration consists of the **import** keyword followed by a fully qualified type name — for import-on-demand declarations the simple type name is replaced by the * character. For example:

```
package demo;
import java.io.DataInputStream;
import java.util.*;
    .
    .
```

The first import declaration imports the `DataInputStream` class from the `java.io` package whilst the second import declaration imports any types from the `java.util` package that are required in this file.

Any imported types can be referenced using their simple type name — this means that an import-single-type declaration must not import a type with the same name as a class or interface already defined by the current package. However, using an import-on-demand declaration to import from a package that defines a type name which is already available (either directly or through an import-single-type declaration) does not cause any problems — the relevant type is simply not imported by the import-on-demand declaration.

10.4 Recursive Programming

The standard `java.util` package provides a number of utility classes but does not include a class to implement the versatile computer data structure known as a 'tree'. As an example of creating a new Java package, the next section describes the `Tree` and `Node` classes and shows how to place these classes in the user-defined `utility` package. The `Tree` and `Node` classes also demonstrate how Java references can be used in the creation of complex data structures — as an introduction this section firstly explains 'hierarchical data structures' and also 'recursive functions'.

In a 'flat data structure' the individual elements are all positioned at the same logical level and they can be reached directly from the 'root' of the data structure. For example, a single-dimensional array is a flat data structure — given the array name each of the elements can be referenced using the `[ ]` subscript operator. The following figure demonstrates the idea for an array `x` containing four elements:

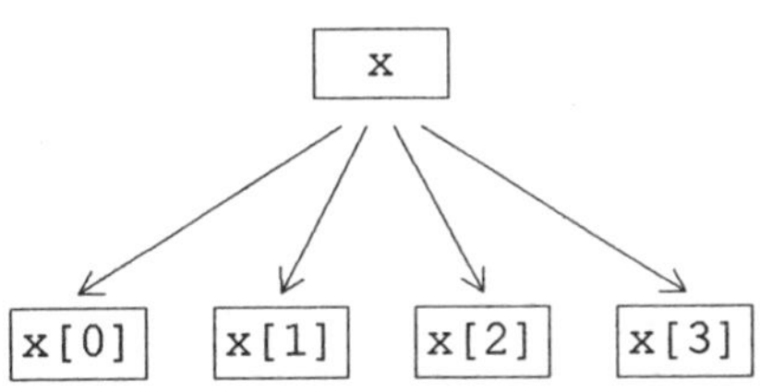

The root of the data structure and the individual elements are collectively known as 'nodes'. In a flat data structure there is a clear distinction between the root node (which represents the whole structure) and the other nodes (which represent individual elements) — however, in a 'hierarchical data structure' this distinction is blurred and any node can act as the root node of a sub-structure. For example, a two-dimensional array may be regarded as a hierarchical data structure — the two-by-two array `x[2][2]` is depicted as such in the following figure:

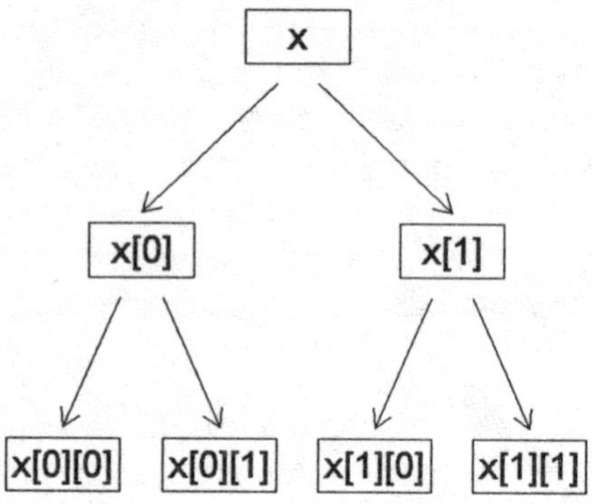

At the top level the root node refers to the array as a whole, at the middle level each node refers to a row within the array and finally at the bottom level each node refers to an element within a row. In other words the root node represents a two-dimensional array, the internal nodes represent one-dimensional arrays and the terminal nodes represent zero-dimensional arrays. So every node represents an array and references sub-arrays within that array — only the dimension of the arrays decreases as the structure is descended. Hence all nodes in a hierarchical structure are in some sense indistinguishable — at every level each node acts as the root of a sub-structure which has essentially the same form as at any other level.

The processing of a hierarchical data structure is often simplified by using 'recursive functions' — in particular, this is true for the tree structures that will be represented by the `Tree` and `Node` classes. A recursive function is one which invokes itself — each recursive function comprises two parts:

1. A nested function call
2. A terminating condition

The first part provides the recursion whilst the second part prevents the function repeatedly invoking itself forever — without the terminating condition the result is 'infinite recursion' and the program thread executing the function will eventually abort with a `StackOverflowError` exception.

A simple example of recursion is the `factorial()` function which calculates the product of its integer argument and all smaller integers:

```
factorial(1) == 1
factorial(2) == 2*1 == 2
factorial(3) == 3*2*1 == 6
factorial(4) == 4*3*2*1 == 24
      .
      .
```

The recursive definition of this function follows:

```
int factorial(int n) {
  if (n == 1)
    return 1;
  return (n*factorial(n-1));
}
```

Now suppose that the function is invoked by the following code:

```
int answer = factorial(4);
```

Here a nested series of calls to the `factorial()` function occurs with `n==4`, `n==3`, `n==2` and finally `n==1`. The results passed back as the nested functions return are `1`, `2`, `6`, and finally `24`.

10.5 Creating a Package

A 'tree' is a classic example of a hierarchical data structure. It has a 'root node' from which branches lead to nodes at the first level, each of these nodes is the root for its own sub-tree and more branches lead to nodes at the second level — the structure is repeated until at the final level are the 'leaf nodes'. A binary tree supports just two branches from each node — the following figure demonstrates the layout of such a tree:

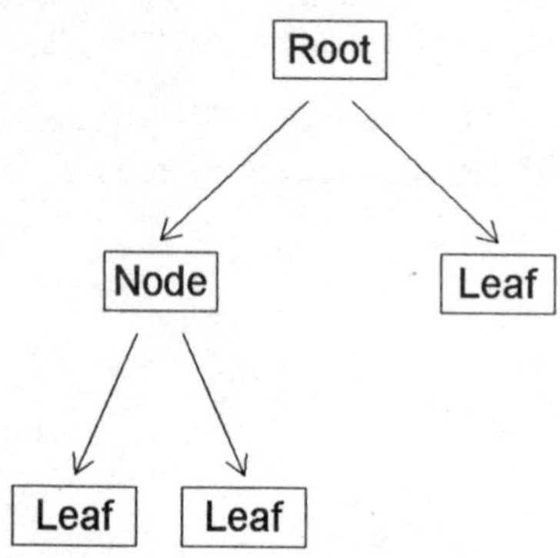

Each node holds references to its left and right sub-trees — either of these references may be `null` to indicate that the sub-tree is empty. If both references are `null` then the node is a leaf node. The `Tree` and `Node` classes will implement a binary tree structure — they are placed in the user-defined `utility` package. The source code for the `Tree` class is defined in the `Tree.java` file:

```
package utility;

public class Tree {
  private Node root;
  public void addNode(Node node) { ... }
        .
        .
}
```

Similarly, the code for the `Node` class appears in the `Node.java` file:

```
package utility;

public class Node {
  private Node left;
  private Node right;
  private int data;
  public Node(int data) { ... }
  void addNode(Node node) { ... }
      .
      .
}
```

The `Tree` class `addNode()` function adds a new `Node` object to the tree:

```
public void addNode(Node node) {
  if (root == null)
    root = node;
  else
    node.addNode(root);
}
```

If the tree is empty then the new node becomes the root node of the tree — otherwise the node is inserted into the tree with a call to the `Node` class `addNode()` function:

```
void addNode(Node node) {
  if (data < node.data)
    if (node.left == null)
      node.left = this;
    else
      addNode(node.left);
  else if (data > node.data)
    if (node.right == null)
      node.right = this;
    else
      addNode(node.right);
}
```

The new node is positioned in the tree according to the integer value stored in its `data` field during construction. If the `data` value is less than that of the root node it will be placed in the left sub-tree of the root — otherwise it will be placed in the right sub-tree of the root. This decision process is applied recursively at each level within the tree — the `Node` class `addNode()` function is therefore easy to implement as a recursive function. The ordering of nodes within the tree allows a particular node to be located easily given the value of its `data` field. It is usually much faster to search a tree structure than to search an array containing the equivalent data elements — this is especially true when the number of elements becomes large.

A new `Node` object is inserted into a tree by passing a reference to the object as a parameter to a `Tree` object's `addNode()` function. The `Tree` class `addNode()` function is declared using the **`public`** keyword and so is available to code outside the `utility` package — on the other hand the `Node` class `addNode()` function has default protection and so cannot be called directly from outside the package. The following code demonstrates how to use the functionality provided by the `utility` package:

```
import utility.*;

Tree tree = new Tree();
tree.addNode(new Node(3));
tree.addNode(new Node(1));
tree.addNode(new Node(4));
tree.addNode(new Node(2));
tree.addNode(new Node(0));
```

Note the use of an import-on-demand declaration to permit the `Tree` and `Node` classes to be referenced using simple names. The code builds the following tree structure:

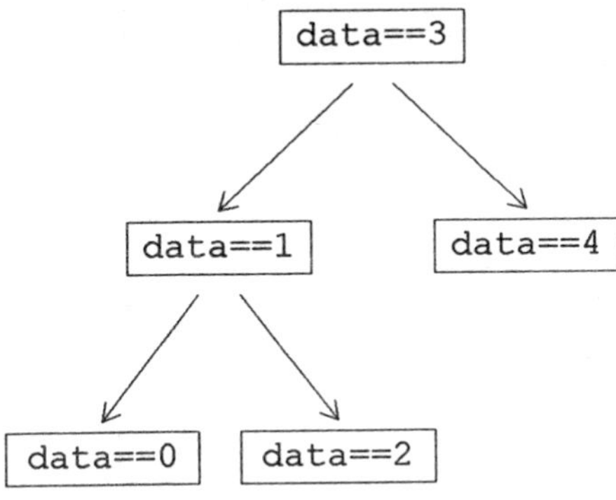

This example shows how easy it is to construct quite complicated data structures using Java references.

10.6 Summary

Java allows classes to be arranged into a hierarchical structure of packages — each package contains a collection of related classes and the hierarchy of packages serves to indicate the logical relation between packages. Java itself defines a series of standard sub-packages belonging to the `java` package — `lang`, `util`, `io`, `awt`, `applet` and `net`. A class or interface can be added to a particular package by adding a package declaration to the file containing the definition of the new Java type. The package declaration must be placed at the start of the file — it is followed by any import declarations and then the class and interface definitions. There are two kinds of import declaration statement (import-single-type and import-on-demand) — both types are used to permit a type defined in another package to be referenced using a simple name. A common policy is to place only a single type definition in each file — indeed in many cases this arrangement is required. A type definition can be assigned a public or default protection level — only public types are available outside the package where they are defined. The availability of individual fields and functions can be further controlled by assigning them to the private, default, protected or public protection levels. In particular, only members assigned to the protected and public levels are available outside the package — public members can be used by any Java code but protected members may only be referenced externally by subclasses that are derived from classes in the package. The chapter also described the process of creating a new user-defined package — the example introduced recursive Java functions and demonstrated the use of Java reference variables in the construction of hierarchical data structures.

11. Fundamental Java Classes

Within the standard `java` package are a number of sub-packages. The most important is the `java.lang` package which contains some fundamental class definitions — the `java.util` package defines a number of additional utility classes. Two notable classes from the `java.lang` package are the `Object` and `Class` classes — every Java class derives from the `Object` class and is represented by a `Class` object. The `java.lang` package also contains the `Process` and `Thread` classes that enable the creation of multi-tasking applications — a multi-threaded approach is less demanding on system resources and is commonly used with Java applets. Synchronized blocks provide one method of synchronizing the activities of several threads and the `Object` class `wait()` and `notify()` functions provide another. Another synchronization mechanism is based on the `Observable` class and the `Observer` interface both from the `java.util` package — an observable object can notify its observers whenever its internal state changes. Other utility classes of interest include the `String`, `StringBuffer` and `Math` classes from the `java.lang` package and also the `Date`, `Random`, `Vector` and `Dictionary` classes defined in the `java.util` package.

11.1 Objects and Classes

There are two classes defined by the `java.lang` package which are fundamental to the Java language — these are the `Object` and `Class` classes. All Java classes are ultimately derived from the `Object` class through the mechanism of inheritance. Every class has an associated `Class` object which describes various properties relating to the class — a `Class` object can also be used to create new objects belonging to the class that it represents.

The `Object` class defines a number of functions that may be inherited by all other Java classes — in particular, all Java arrays inherit the `Object` class functions since each array class has the Object class as its superclass. The Object class equals() function is used to compare two objects:

```
if (x.equals(y)) {
      .
      .
}
```

The equals() function returns true if the x and y variables reference the same object and returns false if they do not. The equals() function is overridden by various subclasses to provide other notions of object equality — for example, the String class defines an equals() function that tests whether two String objects represent the same sequence of characters.

The clone() function provided by the Object class acts in a peculiar manner. It throws an exception of type CloneNotSupportedException unless the object's class supports the Cloneable interface — however, if this interface is indeed supported then the clone() function copies the object's fields to a new object and returns a reference to the new object. In particular, the Object class itself does not implement the Cloneable interface. The clone() function is defined by the Object class and does not belong to the Cloneable interface (which in fact contains no members) — it is therefore possible to override the clone() function and to call the Object class version using the **super** keyword. For example, every array class implements the Cloneable interface and also overrides the clone() function by invoking the superclass version and catching any CloneNotSupportedException exceptions that may be thrown. A function which calls the clone() function for an array is not required to specify this exception type in its **throws** clause if it fails to catch it — however, some Java compilers seem to be unaware of this fact. The Object class clone() function performs a 'shallow copy' of an object — this means that if any of the object's fields are reference variables then the referenced objects are not duplicated. Section 6.2 discusses this point in more detail and provides an example of using the `clone()` function with an array.

The `toString()` function is a particularly important function defined by the `Object` class. The `Object` class version returns a string that includes the actual class of the object plus an object code value — the code value is also available from the `hashCode()` function and is typically the address in memory where the object is stored. However, many classes override the `toString()` function — for example, the version provided by the standard Java class `Date` returns a string denoting the date and time represented by the object.

The `Object` class defines a `finalize()` function — this finalizer performs no action and should be overridden by any classes that require some definite finalization. The `Object` class also defines the `wait()`, `notify()` and `notifyAll()` functions and declares them as final functions so that they cannot be overridden — these functions permit synchronization of different threads and are discussed in section 11.5.

An object can obtain a reference to the `Class` object that represents its class by calling the final `Object` class function `getClass()`. The `Class` object's `getName()` function will supply the name of the object's class — for example:

```
Object x = new Object();
System.out.println(x.getClass().getName());
```

This code will print out the fully qualified class name for the `x` object:

```
java.lang.Object
```

Conversely, the static `Class` function `forName()` returns a `Class` object given just the name of the class — the `newInstance()` function can then be invoked to create an object of the class represented by the `Class` object. For example:

```
Class c = Class.forName("java.util.Date");
Date today = (Date)c.newInstance();
```

In particular, this provides a way of creating objects that belong to a class whose name is not known until run time. The action of the `newInstance()` function is identical to using the **new** keyword but no parameters can be passed to the object constructor.

The `Class` class overrides the `Object` class `toString()` function so that it will supply an object's class name prefixed by the word `class` — if a `Class` object represents an interface rather than a class then the `toString()` function prefixes the interface name with the word `interface` instead. The `isInterface()` function can be used to determine whether a particular `Class` object represents a class or an interface. Finally, the `Class` class also provides a couple of functions for navigating the Java type hierarchy — `getSuperclass()` and `getInterfaces()`. The `getSuperclass()` function returns a new `Class` object representing the superclass of the class associated with the current `Class` object. Similarly, the `getInterfaces()` function returns an array of `Class` objects each representing an interface — these are super-interfaces if the `Class` object represents an interface and they are implemented interfaces if the `Class` object represents a class.

11.2 Strings

The `String` and `StringBuffer` classes are another pair of important classes in the Java language. A `String` object represents a fixed sequence of Java characters — a `StringBuffer` object allows its character sequence to be modified and, in particular, the length of the string need not be constant. A new `String` object can be constructed from a string literal (written in quotes " ") or alternatively copied from another `String` object, or from a `StringBuffer` object or even from a character array. It is also possible to create a new `String` object using the `concat()` function — this works by concatenating the strings held by two existing `String` objects one after the other. For example:

```
String good = "Good";
String bye = "bye!";
System.out.println(good.concat(bye));
```

However, it is often simpler to use the + operator to perform string concatenation. There are also a number of static `valueOf()` functions for creating a `String` object from an expression of an intrinsic type — in most cases these are equivalent to the static `toString()` functions defined by the wrapper classes discussed in the next section. In any case, once a `String` object has been created the length of the string it holds is fixed — the string length can be retrieved using the `String` class `length()` function. The characters in the string are located at positions `0`, `1`, ... up to `length()-1` much like the elements in an array.

The `String` class defines a lot of functions for manipulating strings — some functions process individual characters, some involve substrings and some work with complete strings. A character at a particular position within a string can be retrieved using the `charAt()` function:

```
String s = "Height";
System.out.print(s.charAt(0));
System.out.println(s.charAt(2));
```

Here the message `Hi` is printed by selecting two separate characters from the `String` variable `s`. Conversely, the `indexOf()` function finds the first occurrence of a particular character in a string — if the character is found the function returns the character position, and if not it returns `-1` instead. To look for subsequent occurrences of the character the `indexOf()` function can be provided with a second parameter that specifies the position in the string where the search should begin. Similarly, there are lastIndexOf() functions which scan a string back-to-front looking for a certain character.

The String class also provides functions for manipulating substrings — the two substring() functions create a new String object by taking a sequence of characters from an existing String object. For example:

```
String s = "reaction";
System.out.println(s);
System.out.println(s = s.substring(2));
System.out.println(s.substring(0,3));
```

The first substring() function takes all characters from the specified position up to the end of the string — the second substring() function takes all characters between start (inclusive) and stop (exclusive) positions. Here the code prints the following three lines of text:

```
reaction
action
act
```

The startsWith() and endsWith() functions can be used to determine if one string is a substring of another string — the substring must occur respectively at the start or end of the containing string. A substring at a more general position can be located by passing a String parameter to the indexOf() function — this function returns the position of the substring's first character if the substring is found and returns -1 if it is not.

Finally, the String class defines functions for working with whole strings — there are functions for comparing two strings and functions for converting the characters within a string. The compareTo() function returns a negative, zero or positive result according to the lexical ordering of the two strings that it compares — for example:

```
String[] zoo = {"Monkey","Tiger","Bear"};
for (int i=1; i<zoo.length; i++)
  if (zoo[i-1].compareTo(zoo[i]) < 0)
    System.out.println(zoo[i]);
```

This code prints only the "Tiger" string (and not the "Bear" string). As mentioned earlier the String class equals() function tests for identical strings — the equalsIgnoreCase() function is similar but ignores the case of the characters in the string. The toLowerCase() and toUpperCase() functions generate a new String object from an old one by ensuring that all the characters are either lower or upper case. The replace() function can be used to perform a more general character substitution operation — the function takes two **char** parameters and replaces all occurrences of the first character in the newly created string with the second character.

In contrast to a String object, the character sequence represented by a StringBuffer object is not fixed whenever the object is created — the length of the string is allowed to change and individual characters can be modified. The length() function returns the current length of the string — the setLength() function alters the length of the string by truncation (if the string is shortened) or by the addition of null characters (if the string is lengthened). The charAt() function retrieves the character at a specified position and the setCharAt() function modifies individual characters — the second parameter of the setCharAt() function supplies the replacement character.

The principal functions supplied by the StringBuffer class are the collection of append() and insert() functions. Each append() function accepts a single parameter which is converted to a string and added to the end of the string held by the StringBuffer object. The insert() function is similar to the append() function but it inserts the new string into the middle of the original string instead of placing it at the end — the first parameter specifies the insertion position and the second determines what string to insert. The various append() and insert() functions accept parameters of all intrinsic types (with **byte** and **short** values being converted to **int** type) as well as objects of the `Object` or `String` classes. Finally, the `reverse()` function may be applied to a `StringBuffer` object to reverse the sequence of characters that it holds. For example:

```
StringBuffer s =
  new StringBuffer("!llew");
s.append("eraF").reverse();
System.out.println(s);
```

Here the code constructs the string `"Farewell!"` in the `StringBuffer` object `s` and then prints out this message with an implicit call to the `StringBuffer` class `toString()` function.

11.3 Java Utilities

The standard Java packages provide a number of general utility classes — most of these classes belong to the `java.util` package but the `java.lang` package includes the `Math` class and several 'wrapper classes' that are related to the intrinsic Java data types. The `Math` class defines two mathematical constants (`E` and `PI`) plus a range of common mathematical functions:

Trigonometric Functions and Inverses
: `cos(), sin(), tan(), acos(), asin(), atan()`

Exponential and Logarithmic Functions
: `exp(), log(), pow(), sqrt()`

Rounding Functions
: `ceil(), floor(), rint(), round()`

Assorted other Functions
: `max(), min(), abs(), random()`

Many of these functions accept a single parameter of type **`double`** and return a **`double`** result. However, `round()` converts from **`float`** to **`int`** (or alternatively from **`double`** to **`long`**) by rounding the floating-point value to an integer. Also the `max()` and `min()` functions take two parameters of matching type (**`int`**, **`long`**, **`float`** or **`double`**) and return a result of the same type — the abs() function similarly works with a variety of types but it takes only a single parameter and returns the absolute value. The random() function generates a sequence of pseudo-random numbers of type **double** distributed evenly in the range 0.0 to 1.0 — the Math class actually implements this function by holding a Random object internally. The Random class is defined in the java.util package and provides four different functions yielding evenly-distributed sequences of pseudo-random numbers — nextInt(), nextLong(), nextFloat() and nextDouble(). These sequences can be seeded using the setSeed() function or alternatively the seed can be passed to the Random object constructor — if no seed is explicitly supplied then the constructor generates a seed based on the current time.

The java.lang package also defines a number of wrapper classes — Integer, Long, Double, Float, Character and Boolean. Each object of a wrapper class contains a value of the corresponding intrinsic type — this value is passed to the object's constructor and thereafter cannot be modified. The wrapper classes all define a ...Value() function that retrieves the value held by the object — for example, the Integer class has an intValue() function that returns the wrapped **int** value. In fact the Integer, Long, Double and Float classes are all derived from the abstract Number class and this defines all four intValue(), longValue(), floatValue() and doubleValue() functions. The wrapper classes also provide a number of functions for converting between the intrinsic types and the String class. In particular, all the wrapper classes (except Character) define a static valueOf() function to create a wrapper class object from a string — conversely, all the wrapper classes override the Object class toString() function and the numeric classes also define a static toString() function that accepts values of the corresponding intrinsic types. Finally, the Character class provides several static functions that test for different kinds of character — for example, there are `isDigit()`, `isLetter()` and `isSpace()` functions as well as `isLowerCase()` and `isUpperCase()` functions. The `Character` class also defines the two static functions `toLowerCase()` and `toUpperCase()` — these are similar to the `String` class versions but they work with just a single character.

Section 5.1 introduced the `Date` class defined in the `java.util` package — a simplified user-defined version of the `Date` class is implemented in that section. Each `Date` object represents a date and time accurate to the nearest millisecond — the class provides various `set` and `get` functions to store and retrieve the year, month, day, hour, minute and second values. In particular, the `setDate()` and `getDate()` functions are used to manipulate the day of the month — the `getDay()` function returns the day of the week coded as an integer `0` (Sunday) to `6` (Saturday). If a `Date` object is constructed with no parameters then it represents the date and time of its creation — alternatively, a particular date and time can be passed as constructor arguments. Many of the `Date` class functions are based on the local time zone. However, the time is typically represented internally as the number of milliseconds since `1970 January 1st 00:00:00 GMT` and this is the value manipulated by the `Date` class `setTime()` and `getTime()` functions — the current time is available in this format by calling the `currentTimeMillis()` function of the `System` class. Finally, the `Date` class provides `before()`, `after()` and `equals()` functions to compare the relative ordering of the dates and times represented by a pair of `Date` objects.

The remaining classes in the `java.util` package are mostly 'container classes' that can be used to hold a collection of objects — there are 'dynamic arrays' derived from the `Vector` class and 'associative arrays' derived from the `Dictionary` class. The intrinsic arrays provided by the Java language cannot change in length — however, it is possible to use an existing array reference variable to reference a new array of a different length. The relationship between intrinsic Java arrays and the Vector class is analogous to the relationship between the String and StringBuffer classes — each Vector object acts as a dynamic array that automatically resizes itself whenever new elements are added. The Vector class provides the size() function to report the number of elements currently held by a Vector object — as for intrinsic arrays the elements within a vector are located at positions 0, 1, ... up to size()-1. The isEmpty() function provides a convenient way of testing for zero size. The setSize() function allows the vector size to be modified explicitly — decreasing the size discards objects at the end of the vector and increasing the size adds elements that are initially null.

The array of elements held by a Vector object can be modified using a number of functions. The addElement() function places an object at the end of the array whilst the insertElementAt() puts the new element at a specific position and shuffles the following objects along — both of these functions automatically increase the size of the array by one. The setElementAt() updates a pre-existing element and discards the previous object whilst the removeElementAt() function removes an element and decreases the array size by one. The individual vector elements can be retrieved using the elementAt(), firstElement() and lastElement() functions. The elements() function returns an object supporting the Enumeration interface — this standard Java interface is defined by the java.util package and allows a loop construct to iterate through a collection of objects:

```
Vector x = new Vector();
x.addElement("ready ... ");
x.addElement("steady ... ");
x.addElement("go !!!");
Enumeration e = x.elements();
while (e.hasMoreElements())
  System.out.print(e.nextElement());
System.out.println();
```

The **while** loop prints out the three elements of the x vector to produce the message:

```
ready ... steady ... go !!!
```

The Stack class is derived from the Vector class to implement a 'last-in-first-out' stack — the push() function adds elements to the stack and the pop() function retrieves them in reverse order. The peek() function can be used instead of pop() to obtain a reference to the next object without actually removing the object from the stack.

Associative arrays are implemented by subclasses of the abstract class Dictionary. An associative array differs from an intrinsic Java array in that the elements are selected using objects rather than integers in the range 0 to length-1 — each entry in the associative array consists of an element and a 'key'. The key-element pairs are entered into the array using the put() function — the first parameter of the function defines the key and the second parameter defines the associated element. A particular element can be retrieved from the array by passing the appropriate key to the get() function — this action leaves the entry in the array but the remove() function will discard it. The Dictionary class also defines the keys() and elements() functions — these two functions return objects implementing the Enumeration interface that will iterate through either the keys or the elements in the associative array. The Hashtable class is a non-abstract subclass of the Dictionary class that implements the functionality of an associative array.

The Properties class is a subclass of the Hashtable class that uses only String objects for the keys and elements. A Properties object can be assigned a 'defaults' Properties object that provides values for keys which it does not recognize itself. The Properties class also defines load() and save() functions to permit persistent storage of a Properties object. A set of system properties are available using the getProperties() and getProperty() functions from the System class — these properties provide information on the Java implementation, the underlying operating system and the current user. The getProperties() function returns a Properties object and the getProperty() function looks up individual property strings. The Boolean, Integer and Long wrapper classes respectively define getBoolean(), getInteger() and getLong() functions to read system properties and automatically convert them from strings to **boolean**, Integer or Long types.

11.4 Processes and Threads

Whenever an application needs to perform several activities simultaneously the traditional approach is to run a collection of different 'processes' — each process is fairly independent of the others but they can communicate through various mechanisms such as input/output streams, shared memory or the file system. Indeed Java supports multi-process applications by providing several exec() functions in the System class — invoking an exec() function starts a new process and returns a reference to the associated Process object. The Process object has getInputStream() and getOutputStream() functions for obtaining input/output streams which can be used to communicate with the new process. The exit code generated when the process eventually terminates can be retrieved with the exitValue() function — this function throws an exception if the process is still running and an alternative is to call the waitFor() function which waits for the process to die before returning the exit code. Discarding a Process reference removes only the Process object and does not kill the corresponding process — however, the destroy() function can be used for this purpose.

A more common approach to multi-tasking in Java is to use multiple threads of execution all running in the same process — each thread executes concurrently with all the other threads. This is typically much less demanding on system resources than creating several different processes to do the same work. Each thread shares the resources allocated to its process — for example, if several threads print to the output stream `System.out` then the individual output text will be intermingled. Java provides the `Thread` and `ThreadGroup` classes to accommodate multi-threaded programming — each thread is associated with a `Thread` object and belongs to a thread group represented by a `ThreadGroup` object. The threads and thread groups are arranged into a tree structure — a thread group can contain other thread groups as well as threads. The system thread group appears at the top of the tree. When a program is run it starts with a single thread in some subgroup of the system thread group — if a program creates new threads (or thread groups) then by default these are placed in the same thread group as the current thread. The `Thread` class provides the functions `currentThread()` and `getThreadGroup()` to obtain references for `Thread` and `ThreadGroup` objects — the `ThreadGroup` class provides several functions such as `getParent()`, `threads()` and `groups()` for navigating the thread group tree.

When the number of active threads exceeds the number of processors, 'time-slicing' is used so that the threads still appear to execute concurrently — a thread usually runs until the end of its current time slice and then another thread gets a chance to execute. The individual threads are allocated processor time according to their priorities — a thread's priority can be manipulated using the `Thread` class `getPriority()` and `setPriority()` functions. Usually the thread priorities fall somewhere in the range `MIN_PRIORITY` (1) to `MAX_PRIORITY` (10) but the `ThreadGroup` class `setMaxPriority()` function can be used to further limit the priority values for all threads in a particular thread group (and its subgroups).

There are essentially two ways to start a new thread:

1. subclass the `Thread` class
2. implement the `Runnable` interface

In the first case a new thread class is defined and an object of the class is created. The thread is actually run by invoking the object's `start()` function — for example:

```
MyThread t = new MyThread();
t.start();
```

The current thread returns from the `start()` call and the new thread starts to execute its `run()` function — the `MyThread` class should override the `run()` function to implement the desired functionality. The result is that two threads are now running concurrently.

The second method of creating a new thread is to define a class that implements the `Runnable` interface:

```
class RunObject implements Runnable {
  public void run() {
    System.out.println("I'm a new thread!");
  }
}
```

Now a new `Thread` object is created and passed a reference to an object of the `RunObject` class — this new thread object uses the `RunObject` parameter as its associated 'run object'. As noted above, calling the `start()` function of the `Thread` object starts a new thread and calls its `run()` function — the default action of the `Thread` class `run()` function is to invoke the `run()` function of the associated run object. For example:

```
Thread t = new Thread(new RunObject());
t.start();
```

This code creates a new thread that executes the `RunObject` class `run()` function — hence it prints the message:

```
I'm a new thread!
```

Alas the new thread does not live very long because it terminates when the `run()` function returns.

Whilst a thread is alive it can be halted for a while with the `suspend()` function — the thread can later be allowed to continue by calling the `resume()` function. Both `Thread` and `ThreadGroup` classes define `suspend()` and `resume()` functions — the `Thread` class versions act on a single thread and the `ThreadGroup` functions affect all threads in a thread group (and its subgroups). A thread can temporarily stop executing by calling the `yield()` function and so giving up the remainder of its current time slice — this action schedules another thread for immediate execution. The `sleep()` function is similar but it allows the thread to specify a time period during which it cannot be activated again — alternatively, the `join()` function can be used to make the current thread sleep until some other thread dies. In both cases the sleeping thread can be prematurely awakened by calling the `interrupt()` function of its `Thread` object — the thread returns from the `sleep()` or `join()` function by throwing an `InterruptedException` exception.

To stop the execution of a thread prematurely before it returns from its `run()` function, the `stop()` function of its associated thread object can be invoked. The thread ceases any processing activity it is currently engaged in and then throws a `ThreadDeath` exception. The `ThreadDeath` class is in fact a subclass of `Error` — consequently the `ThreadDeath` exception need not be declared in any **`throws`** lists if it is uncaught. The `ThreadDeath` exception will eventually be handled by the `uncaughtException()` function of the thread group to which the thread belongs — usually the `uncaughtException()` function prints a stack trace to the standard error stream `System.err` but in the case of a `ThreadDeath` exception this is not done. All the threads in a thread group (and its subgroups) can be stopped by calling the `ThreadGroup` class `stop()` function — if necessary the thread group can then be destroyed by the `ThreadGroup` class `destroy()` function.

Whenever all foreground threads have stopped the Java

Virtual Machine that was running them exits — any background (daemon) threads that are still active will be terminated. An alternative method is to call the `System` class `exit()` function — this terminates all remaining threads. The `exit()` function can be passed an integer value that will serve as the exit code for the process — this is the value returned whenever the `Process` class `exitValue()` function is invoked. An exit code of zero conventionally indicates that the process completed without error — this is the value returned if the Virtual Machine exits normally without a call to the `exit()` function.

11.5 Synchronization Mechanisms

Whenever two or more threads share the same data they usually synchronize their actions to avoid unexpected results. For example, without synchronization different threads may observe different variables being updated in a different order — furthermore, if a **`long`** or **`double`** variable is shared then there is the possibility of data corruption unless the threads are synchronized. The simplest method of implementing thread synchronization is to use a sychronized block statement or a synchronized function — these options were introduced in sections 3.2 and 4.1 respectively. In both cases a synchronization object is specified and the thread halts its execution until it can acquire the lock associated with the object — the lock may already be held by another thread that has synchronized on the same object but it will be released automatically whenever the other thread exits its synchronized block. For a synchronized block statement the synchronization object is specified explicitly. For a synchronized function the choice of synchronization object depends on whether the function is static or not — for a non-static function the object is the one executing the function and for a static function the object is the corresponding `Class` object. In any case all variables modified within a synchronized block are updated before the corresponding lock is released — in particular, the synchronization is not limited just to fields of the synchronization object.

A second option for synchronization is to use the `Object` class `wait()` and `notify()` functions. Whereas synchronized blocks are useful in serializing thread manipulations of shared variables, the `wait()` and `notify()` functions are better suited to situations were one thread produces data that is consumed by another. An example of such a 'producer-consumer' relationship is provided by two threads reading a file and processing the data it contains — the producer thread reads the file in large chunks whilst the consumer thread processes the data from previously read chunks. When the consumer has finished its processing it calls the `wait()` function of a synchronization object and then goes to sleep — as soon as the producer has read the next chunk of data it calls the synchronization object's `notify()` function to awaken the consumer. Note that the two processes must acquire the lock associated with the synchronization object before calling the `wait()` and `notify()` functions — in the case of the `wait()` function the lock is automatically released when the thread goes to sleep and later re-acquired before the `wait()` function returns. More than one thread can call the `wait()` function for a particular synchronization object — all such threads are placed in the object's 'wait set'. In this case the `notify()` function picks one thread from the wait set to reawaken — alternatively, the `notifyAll()` function can be called to awaken all the threads at once. Finally, any waiting threads can be interrupted by calling their `interrupt()` functions — as noted in the previous section this abruptly awakens the thread and causes it to throw an `InterruptedException` exception.

The third option for synchronization works with a single thread — it allows one object (observer) to be notified of changes to another object (observable). To support this synchronization mechanism the `java.util` package defines the `Observable` class and the `Observer` interface — an observable object is created from a subclass of `Observable` and an observer object implements the `Observer` interface. The `Observer` interface is an example of the notification interfaces discussed in section 5.4. An observable maintains a list of observers that can be managed by calling the functions `addObserver()` and `deleteObserver()` — both these functions accept an `Observer` reference to identify the observer involved. The observable also contains a boolean flag that can be updated using the `setChanged()` and `clearChanged()` functions to indicate whether the state of the observable object has changed. Whenever the observable's `notifyObservers()` function is called the value of the flag is checked — if the flag is set then it is automatically cleared and all of the observers are notified by calling their `update()` functions. The `update()` function receives two parameters to identify the notification message — the first parameter is an `Observable` reference to the observable object and the second is an `Object` parameter that is passed to the `notifyObservers()` function.

11.6 Summary

The `java.lang` and `java.util` packages provide a variety of useful classes. The two most important classes are `Object` and `Class` — every Java class is derived from the `Object` class and is described by a `Class` object. The `String` and `StringBuffer` classes are another pair of common classes — each `String` object represents an immutable character string but the `StringBuffer` class provides a collection of `append()` and `insert()` functions for modifying a string. Java also supplies a large number of utility classes. There are wrapper classes (`Integer`, `Long`, `Float`, `Double`, `Character` and `Boolean`) for all the intrinsic types — each wrapper object holds an intrinsic value of the corresponding type. The wrapper classes also define functions to perform conversions between intrinsic types and strings. The `Math` class provides a variety of mathematical constants and functions — the `Random` class generates sequences of pseudo-random numbers. A `Date` object can be used to represent a date and time in the local time zone — the current time is available by creating a

Date object with no parameters. There are also several container classes derived from the Vector class (dynamic arrays) and from the Dictionary class (associative arrays) — the Enumeration interface provides a way to iterate through all the elements contained in these arrays. To support applications that must perform multi-tasking Java provides the Process and Thread classes — using multiple threads within a single process is generally preferred to creating several different processes. There are two ways of creating a new thread — subclassing the Thread class or implementing the Runnable interface. In either case the thread is started by calling the Thread class start() function — this executes the run() function of the thread object or its associated run object. The new thread continues to live until it returns from the run() function — the stop() function of the associated Thread object can be invoked to terminate the thread prematurely. The activities of several different threads can be synchronized using synchronized blocks or alternatively with the Object class wait() and notify() functions. A final synchronization mechanism is provided by the Observable class and the Observer interface — an observable object is able to notify its observers whenever there is a change to its internal state.

12. Input/Output Processing

Another useful sub-package of the `java` package is the `java.io` package — this provides classes for handling input and output data streams and for manipulating files and the file system. Most of the Java stream classes are derived from the abstract classes `InputStream` and `OutputStream` — these classes declare `read()` and `write()` functions for inputting and outputting data as a series of 8-bit bytes. There are two sets of classes derived from these basic stream classes that work with Java pipes (`PipedInputStream` and `PipedOutputStream`) and also with sequential files (`FileInputStream` and `FileOutputStream`). The subclasses derived from the `FilterInputStream` and `FilterOutputStream` classes allow the data in a stream to be processed in some way — this 'filtering' operation may simply add functionality to the stream (such as buffering the data or maintaining a line number count) or it may modify the data before it is transferred. The `PrintStream` class is a useful filtered stream class that allows a variety of data types to be printed easily. Java also provides the `DataInput` and `DataOutput` interfaces that define a collection of functions for handling streams containing formatted data — the `DataInputStream` and `DataOutputStream` classes each implement one of these interfaces. The class `RandomAccessFile` implements both `DataInput` and `DataOutput` interfaces — it also provides a file pointer to permit manipulation of a file in a non-sequential manner. Finally, the `File` class is defined by the `java.io` package for managing files and directories in the file system.

12.1 Data Streams

Input/output processing in Java is principally based on the use of byte streams. Indeed nearly all of the standard Java input/output classes are derived from the two abstract classes `InputStream` and `OutputStream` — the basic `read()` and `write()` functions declared by these classes transfer information to and from a Java program as a sequence of 8-bit bytes. In particular, streams can be used to transfer data between the program and the user (via the keyboard and the screen) or alternatively to and from files in the file system — it is also possible for one thread to write data to one stream and for a second thread to read the 'piped' data from another stream. Section 12.3 looks at Java pipes whilst sections 12.7 and 12.8 deal with file-related streams.

The `FilterInputStream` and `FilterOutputStream` classes are derived from the classes `InputStream` and `OutputStream` respectively. These two subclasses are designed to allow the embedding of an unfiltered stream within an object from a filtered stream class — the data from the embedded stream is processed by the embedding object before it is transferred. Some useful subclasses of `FilterInputStream` and `FilterOutputStream` are discussed in sections 12.4 and 12.5. In particular, `DataInputStream` and `DataOutputStream` are filtered stream classes which respectively implement the `DataInput` and `DataOutput` interfaces — these two interfaces are needed when formatted data streams are involved. Similarly, the `PrintStream` class is another filtered stream class that allows many different data formats to be printed easily — the `System.out` stream used extensively in earlier chapters is a `PrintStream` object.

Most errors that can occur with the standard Java input/output streams are reported by throwing an exception of the `IOException` class or one of its sub-classes — this exception must be explicitly caught or alternatively added to a function's **`throws`** list.

12.2 Basic Input/Output

The Java stream system is based on the two abstract classes `InputStream` and `OutputStream`. The standard Java stream classes override the abstract `read()` and `write()` functions declared by these superclasses for transferring a single byte of data — there are also a number of other basic stream functions which may be overridden and, of course, extra functionality can be added by the various subclasses.

The `InputStream` class defines `read()` functions for inputting one byte or an array of bytes. These two functions block until a byte of data has been read or an error is encountered — upon return the latter function provides the actual number of bytes read and both functions return a value of `-1` to indicate that no more bytes are available from this stream. There is also a `skip()` function that can be used to skip past a number of unwanted bytes — the function may skip fewer bytes than requested and the number actually skipped is returned as the result of the function. The `available()` function can be called to determine the number of bytes which can be read or skipped without the input function blocking and waiting for more data to arrive.

The `OutputStream` class similarly defines `write()` functions for outputting a single byte or an array of bytes. There is also an `OutputStream` class `flush()` function that flushes any written bytes that have been buffered by the output stream.

The `InputStream` class defines `mark()` and `reset()` functions. The `mark()` function is called to mark a specific point in the stream of incoming bytes and the `reset()` function returns the stream to this mark so that a number of bytes can be re-read — the `mark()` function passes a value to indicate the maximum number of bytes that should be saved. The `markSupported()` function returns true only if the `mark()-reset()` functionality is supported — in particular, the `InputStream` class version of this function returns `false`.

Finally, both the `InputStream` and `OutputStream` classes define a `close()` function to close an input/output stream — a closed stream cannot read or write any more data and cannot be re-opened.

12.3 Pipes

A Java pipe provides a mechanism for transferring data from one thread to another — one of the threads writes data to an output stream and the other reads the piped data from an input stream. The `PipedOutputStream` and `PipedInputStream` classes are defined to support the use of pipes — the writer stream creates an object of the former class and the reader stream creates an object of the latter. Before data can be transferred through the pipe it is first necessary to connect the output stream to the input stream — both `PipedOutputStream` and `PipedInputStream` classes provide a `connect()` function for this purpose. Only one of the `connect()` functions needs to be called — either the output stream reference is passed as a parameter to the input stream function or vice versa. After connecting the pipe the threads can transfer data with the `read()` and `write()` functions — the piped data is buffered so that the input thread will block until new data arrives in the buffer and the output thread will block if the buffer becomes full. Whenever the output thread has finished writing all its data it calls the `close()` function and the input thread will eventually receive the end-of-stream value (`-1`) when it calls the `read()` function. The following code is typical for the writer thread:

```
PipedOutputStream out_pipe =
         new PipedOutputStream();
Reader reader = new Reader(out_pipe);
Thread t = new Thread(reader);
t.start();
synchronized (reader) {
  reader.wait();
}
int data = 0;
while ((data=in.read()) != -1)
  out_pipe.write(data);
out_pipe.close();
```

Here a Reader object is created and passed a reference to the piped output stream — a new thread is created to run the Reader object. The writer thread then waits until the reader thread signals that it has connected to the other end of the pipe. Finally, all the data from some input stream in is transferred through the pipe and then the output stream is closed.

The constructor of the Reader object saves the reference to the piped output stream:

```
Reader(PipedOutputStream out_pipe) {
  this.out_pipe = out_pipe;
}
```

Whenever the reader thread is started the Reader object's run() function executes the following code:

```
PipedInputStream in_pipe =
         new PipedInputStream();
in_pipe.connect(out_pipe);
synchronized (this) {
  notify();
}
int data = 0;
while ((data=in_pipe.read()) != -1) {
  // process data
}
in_pipe.close();
```

The function creates the piped input stream and then connects both ends of the pipe — it calls the notify() function to signal to the writer thread that it is ready to receive data.

12.4 Filtered Input/Output

Java provides a number of ways of modifying the basic input/output mechanism provided by the InputStream and OutputStream classes. For example, the SequenceInputStream class allows a number of input streams to be concatenated. The SequenceInputStream constructor is supplied with an `Enumeration` object that will iterate through a set of streams — data is read from one stream after another until the sequence is exhausted. Several other filter classes are derived from the `FilterInputStream` and `FilterOutputStream` classes — these superclasses are themselves subclasses of the `InputStream` and `OutputStream` classes respectively. Both `FilterInputStream` and `FilterOutputStream` classes define a field to hold an embedded stream object belonging to their superclass — this stream is passed as a constructor parameter and calls to the various input/output functions of the filtered stream object are simply passed along to the embedded stream.

The other filtered stream classes are derived from `FilterInputStream` and `FilterOutputStream` and they add extra functionality to the embedded stream. For example, the `PushbackInputStream` class allows a single character to be read and then pushed back into the stream for re-reading later — also the `LineNumberInputStream` class counts the number of line terminators (`'\r'` or `'\n'` or `'\r'` followed immediately by `'\n'`), converts each one to a newline character and provides the current line count with the `getLineNumber()` function. The classes `BufferedInputStream` and `BufferedOutputStream` are another two filtered stream classes — they use a buffer (of default size 512 bytes) so that the underlying operating can increase efficiency by performing input/output operations on large blocks of data. The buffer is implemented using `buf`, `count` and `pos` fields — the `buf` array holds the buffered data, the `count` field indicates the amount of data held and the `pos` field is used by the `BufferedInputStream` class to locate the next byte to read. Furthermore, the `BufferedInputStream` class always supports the `mark()-reset()` functionality discussed in section 12.2. The next section covers three more standard filtered stream classes (`PrintStream`, `DataInputStream` and `DataOutputStream`) which work with formatted data streams.

12.5 Formatted Streams

The `PrintStream` class allows a variety of different data types to be printed in a straightforward manner — an example of the `PrintStream` class which appears throughout this book is the `System.out` stream that connects to the computer screen. The `PrintStream` class defines the `print()` and `println()` functions to perform the formatted output — the only difference between the pair of functions is that the latter appends a newline character (`'\n'`) to anything else that is printed. Both functions are overloaded to accept a variety of arguments — all the intrinsic types are accepted (with **`byte`** and **`short`** being converted to **`int`** type) as well as references to `Object` and `String` classes. The data is printed in an easy-to-read format which is generally the same as that obtained from the corresponding `String.valueOf()` function. If the `println()` function is invoked without a parameter then a blank line is displayed. Another feature of the `PrintStream` class is that the stream can be set to autoflush whenever a newline character is sent to the stream — a flag passed to the stream constructor turns on the autoflush behaviour. The `PrintStream` class never throws an `IOException` but instead sets an internal flag if any errors are encountered — this flag can be examined by calling the `checkError()` function.

The `DataInput` and `DataOutput` interfaces are implemented by classes that represent formatted data streams — in particular, these interfaces are implemented by the standard Java classes `DataInputStream` and `DataOutputStream`. The `DataOutput` functions write data that is acceptable to a `DataInput` stream — there are functions for reading and writing all of the intrinsic types. However, the `writeByte()`, `writeShort()` and `writeChar()` functions all take a parameter of **`int`** type — furthermore, there are `readUnsignedByte()` and `readUnsignedShort()` alternatives to the `readByte()` and `readShort()` functions and the unsigned variants return an **int** value. The DataInput and DataOutput interfaces also define a few functions that treat the stream as essentially unformatted byte data. The DataOutput interface has write() functions for outputting a single byte or an array of bytes that are identical to the OutputStream versions — there are also writeBytes() and writeChars() functions that convert a String object to a series of bytes using the writeByte() and writeChar() functions. The DataInput interface has readFully() and readLine() functions — the readFully() function blocks until its byte array parameter can be filled (whereas the corresponding InputStream class read() function may return with fewer bytes than requested) and the readLine() function returns a full line of input (including any line terminator characters) as a String object. There is also a DataInput interface skipBytes() function that is practically identical to the InputStream class skip() function.

The DataInputStream and DataOutputStream classes respectively implement the DataInput and DataOutput interfaces. These filtered stream classes allow an unformatted input/output stream to be converted to a formatted one — a common example is the creation of a DataInputStream object from the System.in stream:

```
DataInputStream data =
     new DataInputStream(System.in);
int i = Integer.parseInt(data.readLine());
```

The DataOutputStream class has a written field that contains a count of the number of bytes written to the stream — this field is protected but its value is available by calling the size() function.

12.6 The File System

One of the design principles for the Java language is security — in particular, this means that the Java applets discussed in chapter 14 are generally forbidden use of the file system by the Web browser that is running them. However, for full Java applications such as a server program that communicates with a collection of applets the file system provides a good place to store persistent data. The exact operation of the Java classes dealing with the file system are to some extent dependent on the underlying operating system — however, Java does generally manage to achieve its other design goal of portability.

The `File` class is used to create objects that represent individual files and directories in the file system — each `File` object holds the pathname of the associated file or directory. A new `File` object can be constructed by specifying the pathname as a single `String` argument or alternatively the pathname can be supplied as separate directory and file components — the `File` class `separatorChar` field contains the character that will be used to concatenate the two components. The `getPath()` function returns a `File` object's pathname whilst the `getParent()` and `getName()` functions respectively return the directory and file (or sub-directory) components. Both 'absolute' and 'relative' pathnames are allowed but the meanings of these terms are operating system dependent — the `isAbsolute()` function tests whether a `File` object represents an absolute pathname and the function `getAbsolutePath()` converts a pathname to absolute form before returning the result as a `String` object.

A new file is typically created by opening a file-related stream as discussed in the next two sections — the `File` class `mkdir()` function creates a new directory using the pathname held by a `File` object and the `mkdirs()` function also creates any necessary parent directories. The files in a particular directory can be listed by calling the `list()` function for a `File` object that represents the directory — this function returns an array of `String` objects. The `File` class `renameTo()` and `delete()` functions allow a file or directory to be moved or deleted.

The `File` class also defines a series of functions for testing the properties of the file or directory associated with a particular `File` object — the `isFile()` and `isDirectory()` functions determine whether a file or a directory is involved. The `exists()` function tests whether the file or directory actually exists in the file system and if it does then the `canRead()` and `canWrite()` functions indicate whether it can be read or written. The `length()` function returns the size of a file in bytes and the `lastModified()` function indicates when a file or directory was last modified.

12.7 Sequential Files

The `FileInputStream` and `FileOutputStream` classes are derived from the classes `InputStream` and `OutputStream` respectively — they allow a file to be read or written as a serial stream of bytes using the basic stream `read()` and `write()` functions. The next section describes the `RandomAccessFile` class which allows for somewhat more sophisticated file processing. A `FileInputStream` or `FileOutputStream` object can be created by passing the constructor one of the three following items:

1. a `String` object
2. a `File` object
3. a `FileDescriptor` object

The first two options specify a pathname for the file involved and a `FileNotFoundException` exception is thrown if the file cannot be opened — if the function succeeds then a `FileDescriptor` object is created internally to describe the connection to the file. Whereas a `File` object can contain the pathname of a file that may or may not exist, a valid `FileDescriptor` object always refers to an actual file. The third option for constructing a new file stream object uses an existing connection to the required file. In any case the `FileDescriptor` object associated with a `FileInputStream` or `FileOutputStream` object may be retrieved by calling the `getFD()` function. A file is closed using the inherited close() function — alternatively, the file stream classes define finalizer functions to clean up connections to any files that are not explicitly closed.

12.8 Random Access Files

The RandomAccessFile class is designed to manipulate data at non-sequential positions within a file — it also implements both the DataInput and DataOutput interfaces described in section 12.5 so that formatted data structures can be created within the file. The class is not derived from either of the InputStream or OutputStream classes but it does define read() functions that act like the InputStream versions.

A RandomAccessFile object can be created by passing the constructor the pathname of a file using either a String or a File object — the RandomAccessFile object creates a FileDescriptor object internally and this can be retrieved with the getFD() function. The constructor must also be passed a string (either "r" or "rw") to specify whether the file should be opened read-only or alternatively for both read and write operations.

Each RandomAccessFile object has an associated 'file pointer' that locates the position within the file where the next byte will be written or read — the current value of the file pointer is returned by the getFilePointer() function. The file pointer moves automatically whenever bytes are transferred to or from the file — alternatively the file pointer can be positioned explicitly using the seek() function. To move to the end of the file the length() function can be called to determine the file size — for example:

```
long end_of_file = file.length();
file.seek(end_of_file);
```

When all the necessary read/write operations have been completed then the file can be closed by calling the RandomAccessFile class close() function.

12.9 Summary

Java bases its input/output processing on byte streams. The basic stream functionality is defined by the abstract `InputStream` and `OutputStream` classes — most of the standard Java stream classes are derived from these two classes. In particular, the `InputStream` and `OutputStream` classes define `read()` and `write()` functions that transfer a single byte or an array of bytes — both classes define a `close()` function that can be called whenever a stream is no longer needed for input/output. The `InputStream` class also defines `mark()` and `reset()` functions that can be used to re-read a portion of the input stream data — on the other hand, the `OutputStream` class has a `flush()` function to send any buffered data on its way. The `PipedInputStream` and `PipedOutputStream` classes are subclasses of the basic Java stream classes that allow two threads to communicate by sending data through a pipe — the pipe stream classes both define a `connect()` function that can be used to connect the two ends of the pipe. The `FileInputStream` and `FileOutputStream` classes are another pair of subclasses of the basic stream classes — they are used to transfer a serial stream of bytes between the program and some file in the file system. Individual files and directories can also be manipulated using objects of the `File` class — each `File` object holds the pathname of the associated file or directory. To perform input/output operations on a file in a non-sequential manner Java provides the `RandomAccessFile` class that defines a file pointer which can be moved to an arbitrary position within a file — the class also implements the `DataInput` and `DataOutput` interfaces. The `DataInput` interface defines a series of functions such as `readChar()`, `readInt()` and `readFloat()` for reading formatted data from a stream — the `DataOutput` interface defines a corresponding set of functions for writing data to a stream in a compatible format. The `FilterInputStream` and `FilterOutputStream` classes allow one stream to be embedded by another — for subclasses of the basic filtered stream classes, the embedding object filters the data passing through the embedded stream before transferring it. The `BufferedInputStream` and `BufferedOutputStream` classes are examples of derived filtered stream classes — they use an internal buffer to assist the underlying operating system in transferring stream data more efficiently using large blocks. The classes `DataInputStream` and `DataOutputStream` are another pair of filtered stream classes — they respectively implement the `DataInput` and `DataOutput` interfaces and so can be used with formatted data streams. Finally, the `PrintStream` class defines the `print()` and `println()` functions to allow simple output of a variety of data types in user-readable form.

13. Abstract Window Toolkit

Java programs may be run in many different computing environments — the `java.awt` (Abstact Window Toolkit) package helps to provide a standardized means of controlling window-based applications. The Java windowing system is based on the abstract `Component` class whose subclasses implement various window components such as buttons, labels, scrollbars and list boxes. The `Container` class is an abstract subclass of `Component` from which all window container classes are derived. The container classes implement components such as top-level windows, dialog boxes and applets within which other sub-components can be placed — a container typically uses a layout manager to determine how its components are to be arranged. Java notifies a program of user input by sending `Event` objects to the components over which these events occur — similarly, Java invokes a component's `paint()` function whenever its contents need to be redrawn. The use of images in Java is based on the `Image` class — there are also a number of image-related classes and interfaces in the `java.awt.image` package. In particular, this package contains support for image producers, image consumers, image observers and image filters. An image producer supplies an image to an image consumer whilst an image filter can modify the image data in transit — an image observer is informed of progress whenever an `Image` object loads an image. Finally, the `java.awt.image` package also defines two important types of colour model — a colour model is used to determine the actual colours of the pixels within an image.

13.1 Windows Programming

A window-based application provides a graphical user interface — the actions of such a program are driven by a sequence of events (such as key presses or mouse clicks) that are generated by the user. The Java windowing system is based on the `Component` class and its subclass `Container` — a `Component` object is associated with a basic window item such as a button or a scrollbar whilst a `Container` object represents a container (such as a window or dialog box) within which a number of components can be laid out. In particular, the `Component` and `Container` classes provide the `deliverEvent()`, `postEvent()` and `handleEvent()` functions for handling the `Event` objects which describe the various events produced by user interaction. The `deliverEvent()` function determines which window component the event belongs to and if necessary translates the mouse coordinates so that the origin of the coordinate system is located at the top-left hand corner of the component — the `x`- and `y`-coordinates increase from left to right and from top to bottom respectively. The `postEvent()` function is then called for the appropriate component and this in turn invokes the `handleEvent()` function — if the `handleEvent()` function returns `true` then the event has been processed but if it returns `false` then the event must be posted to the component's container (or for top-level popup windows to the main window). This allows individual events to be handled by the components to which they are originally delivered or alternatively a container can process all events sent to the components which it contains. The default `handleEvent()` function provided by the `Component` class returns `false` immediately unless the event is one of the following types:

Action Event
: `action()`

Focus Event
: `gotFocus()` or `lostFocus()`

Key Event
: `keyDown()` or `keyUp()`

Mouse Event
: `mouseEnter()`, `mouseExit()`, `mouseMove()`, `mouseDrag()`, `mouseDown()` or `mouseUp()`

In this case the `handleEvent()` function calls one of the other functions indicated and uses the result as its own return value — all the `Component` class event functions return `false`. Each of the event functions is passed the `Event` object from the `handleEvent()` call as its first argument. The `action()` function and the focus event functions receive a second `Object` parameter to further describe the event. An action event occurs when the user signals that some action is required by, for example, setting a check box or selecting a menu item — the focus events occur when the keyboard focus moves to a new component. The key event functions are instead passed an **`int`** as their second parameter — this is set to the character of the key pressed or released. Finally, the mouse event functions receive the mouse coordinates as a pair of **`int`** parameters.

Each `Event` object contains a number of fields that specify the type of event and also provide additional information. The object representing the component associated with an event is placed in the `Event` object's `target` field. The `id` field identifies the event type and can take the following values:

1. `ACTION_EVENT`
2. `GOT_FOCUS` or `LOST_FOCUS`
3. `KEY_PRESS`, `KEY_RELEASE`, `KEY_ACTION` or `KEY_ACTION_RELEASE`
4. `MOUSE_ENTER`, `MOUSE_EXIT`, `MOUSE_MOVE`, `MOUSE_DRAG`, `MOUSE_DOWN` or `MOUSE_UP`

There are also several other event types associated with particular window components such as scrollbars, list boxes or windows. Depending on the type of event the `arg` field may contain an object (such as a `String` object) that provides additional information relating to the event. For key events the `key` field contains the relevant key character — `KEY_ACTION` and `KEY_ACTION_RELEASE` events use a number of predefined key constants such as `HOME`, `F1` or `PGUP`. For mouse events the `x` and `y` fields hold the mouse coordinates — double clicks can be detected by testing the `clickCount` field for a value greater than one. The modifiers field is set for key events to indicate the state of the modifier keys using the flags SHIFT_MASK, CTRL_MASK, ALT_MASK and META_MASK — for mouse events the ALT_MASK and META_MASK flags respectively indicate that the middle or right buttons have been pressed. Finally, the when field provides a time-stamp for the event.

To customize the behaviour of a component its standard Java class must be subclassed and the relevant event functions should then be overridden by the derived class. For common events this usually involves one of the specialized event functions but sometimes it is necessary to override the handleEvent() function — in the latter case a call to the superclass handleEvent() function is needed to handle all remaining events. For example:

```
public class MyFrame extends Frame {
  public boolean handleEvent(Event e) {
    if (e.target == this &&
          e.id == Event.WINDOW_DESTROY) {
      dispose();
      return true;
    }
    return super.handleEvent(e);
  }
}
```

A Frame object represents a top-level window with a border and title bar — section 13.4 discusses the Frame class in more detail. The MyFrame subclass overrides the handleEvent() function and looks for the arrival of a WINDOW_DESTROY event indicating that the user has requested closure of the window — the dispose() function is called to destroy the window and release any resources that it was using. All other events delivered to the frame window are passed to the Frame superclass for further processing.

Java also defines a Toolkit class that is used in the creation of actual implementations of the Abstract Window

Toolkit — most applications do not need to concern themselves with the `Toolkit` class or with the associated component peer interfaces defined in the `java.awt.peer` package.

13.2 Graphics and Text

Some user-defined component classes allow the program to draw directly to a rectangular area within a window — these classes are derived from a standard Java class and place their drawing code inside overridden versions of the `update()` or `paint()` functions. In particular, this technique is applicable to the `Applet` class described in the next chapter.

A component's `paint()` function is called initially to set up the contents of its drawable area and may be called again later if the area is hidden by other windows and then re-exposed. Alternatively, the program can explicitly request that a component be redrawn by calling its `repaint()` function — this asks Java to call the component's `update()` function as soon as possible and the `update()` function typically invokes the `paint()` function. The `update()` function receives a `Graphics` object as a parameter which represents a 'graphics context' for the drawable area — the graphics context holds a variety of default values that determine how various drawing operations are performed. In particular, the graphics context sets the current colour and the current font and it also fixes the origin of the coordinate system and the clipping rectangle outside which no drawing takes place — the origin is usually at the top-left corner of the component and the clipping rectangle extends to the edges of the component. The `Component` version of the `update()` function erases the contents of the component with the background colour — it then sets the current colour of its `Graphics` object to the component's foreground colour and finally invokes the `paint()` function, passing along the `Graphics` object. Hence a derived class should override the `update()` function or the `paint()` function as appropriate — the former option is preferred if the automatic erasure of the component's contents is not required. For example:

```
public class MyCanvas extends Canvas {
  public void paint(Graphics g) {
    Dimension d = size();
    FontMetrics fm = g.getFontMetrics();
    int width = fm.stringWidth("Hello!");
    int x = (d.width-width)/2;
    int y = d.height/2;
    g.drawString("Hello!",x,y);
  }
}
```

The `Canvas` class is one component class that allows the program to draw directly to a window — the `MyCanvas` subclass overrides the `paint()` function to draw the `"Hello!"` string in the middle of the component. The `Component` class `size()` function returns the width and height of the canvas as a `Dimension` object — the graphics context supplies a `FontMetrics` object for the current font and this is used to calculate the width of the string. The `Graphics` class `drawString()` function is passed `x` and `y` coordinates to specify the baseline for the text and the start position on this baseline.

The `Graphics` class defines a whole host of functions for dealing with graphics and text whilst the `Font` and `FontMetrics` classes are especially designed to handle a variety of different character fonts. There are also several utility classes for representing points and dimensions — `Point`, `Dimension`, `Insets`, `Rectangle` and `Polygon`.

The `Graphics` class provides the `setColor()` and `getColor()` functions for managing the current colour of the graphics context — the colour is specified using the `Color` class described in section 13.9. Similarly, there are `Graphics` class `setFont()` and `getFont()` functions for manipulating the current font — as noted above there is also a `getFontMetrics()` function for obtaining the

FontMetrics object that describes various properties of the current font. The drawString() function allows a string to be drawn at a certain location within the component — there are also drawBytes() and drawChars() variants that supply the string as an array of bytes or characters. The Graphics class also provides functions for drawing various geometrical shapes — for example, drawLine() connects two end points, drawOval() and drawArc() respectively draw a complete ellipse or part of one, drawRect() produces a rectangle and the drawPolygon() function can be used for more general polygons. There are corresponding fill functions that fill the interior of a closed shape with the current foreground colour — there is also a clearRect() function that fills a rectangle with the component's background colour. Finally, the Graphics class defines several versions of the drawImage() function for drawing the image associated with an Image object — the use of images in Java is introduced in section 13.7.

A Font object is used to represent a particular character font — a new object can be constructed by passing the font name, style (PLAIN, BOLD or ITALIC) and size (in points). A FontMetrics object describes the dimensions of the characters which constitute the associated font. In particular, the charWidth() function returns the width needed to draw a certain character whilst the stringWidth() function is the equivalent for strings — there are also bytesWidth() and charsWidth() variants of the latter function that permit a string to be specified as an array of bytes or characters. Characters are aligned relative to a horizontal baseline — the ascent and descent metrics describe how far a character extends above or below this baseline. The FontMetrics class getAscent() and getDescent() functions return sensible values for these quantities which can be used to set the interline spacing — alternatively the getHeight() function returns the sum of these two values plus the additional padding recommended by the getLeading() function.

The `Point` class represents 2-dimensional points. It has public fields `x` and `y` that are set by the constructor or the `move()` function — there is also a `translate()` function to update the point. Similarly, the `Dimension` class represents the size of 2-dimensional objects with its public `height` and `width` fields. The `Insets` class is used to describe the placement of one component within another — the public fields `left`, `right`, `top` and `bottom` indicate the size of the border around the inner component. The `Rectangle` class has public fields `x`, `y`, `width` and `height` to represent a rectangle — there are a number of ways of constructing a `Rectangle` including, for example, from a `Point` object and a `Dimension` object. The `Rectangle` class also defines several functions for manipulating a rectangle. There are `move()` and `translate()` functions for moving a rectangle to a new position, a `resize()` function for changing the size of the rectangle and a `reshape()` function for performing both operations simultaneously — there is also a `grow()` function that moves all four sides of the rectangle outwards (or inwards if negative parameters are passed). The `inside()` function tests whether a particular point is inside the rectangle and if necessary the `add()` function can be used to increase the size of the rectangle just enough to include the point. The `union()` and `intersection()` functions respectively create the union and intersection rectangles of two existing rectangles. The `intersects()` function tests whether the intersection rectangle is empty or not — an alternative is to use the `isEmpty()` function.

Finally, the `Polygon` class represents a more general polygon — the points of the polygon are stored in the public array fields `xpoints` and `ypoints` with the size of the array appearing in the public `npoints` field. The `Polygon` object can be created by passing the points to the constructor or alternatively the points can be added using the `addPoint()` function. The `inside()` function tests if a point is inside the polygon using the 'odd-even' rule and the `getBoundingBox()` function returns a `Rectangle` object representing a rectangle that just encompasses the polygon.

13.3 Component Classes

The `Component` class is the abstract superclass of nearly all window components — menu component classes inherit instead from the `MenuComponent` class. Many of the `Component` class functions have already been discussed in the previous two sections — in particular, the `Component` class has several functions relating to user events, several more involved with repainting a component, and yet others used for displaying images (see section 13.7). There are also functions to modify the position and size of a component — the `move()` function changes the position, the `resize()` function alters the size and the `reshape()` function does both. However, these functions are usually only used with top-level windows (or applets) since all sub-components within a container are laid out automatically by the container's layout manager — section 13.5 discusses the operation of a layout manager in more detail. The `Component` class `size()` function supplies the current size of a component and the `bounds()` function returns its bounding rectangle. There are also `setForeground()` and `setBackground()` functions for updating the component's foreground and background colours — similarly there are `getForeground()` and `getBackground()` functions for retrieving the current colour values. The `setFont()` and `getFont()` functions manipulate the current font. The `getGraphics()` function supplies a `Graphics` object for the component — this is most useful for off-screen images since the `update()` or `paint()` function typically supplies the `Graphics` object for an on-screen component. Finally, the `disable()` and `enable()` functions can be used to control which components accept user input — similarly, the `hide()` and `show()` functions determine whether a component is visible or not. The `isEnabled()` and `isVisible()` functions test the current status of a component.

The previous section introduced the `Canvas` class — this is one of the simplest component classes and by default it just paints a rectangle in the component's background colour. A subclass overrides the `Canvas` class `paint()` function to draw a particular design on the canvas — an alternative is to override the inherited `update()` function. A `Canvas` component can also be used to receive input from the user — for example, mouse clicking over the canvas may be used to request some action.

Another `Component` subclass is the `Label` class — this represents a label component that contains text which the user cannot edit. A `Label` object constructor can specify the label text string and also the text justification (`CENTER`, `LEFT` or `RIGHT`) — the `setText()` and `getText()` functions are available to later manipulate the label text whilst the `setAlignment()` and `getAlignment()` functions determine the alignment. The `TextField` and `TextArea` classes are subclasses of the `TextComponent` class — a `TextField` object allows only a single line of text to be displayed whilst a `TextArea` object supports a multi-line text format. The `TextComponent` superclass defines `setText()` and `getText()` functions for transferring all the text held by the component — the `setEditable()` and `isEditable()` functions determine whether the text can be edited by the user. The class also permits a section of the text to be selected either by the user or with the `select()` and `selectAll()` functions — the extent of the current selection can be obtained using the `getSelectionStart()` and `getSelectionEnd()` functions or alternatively `getSelectedText()` returns the selected text. A `TextField` object constructor may be passed the initial contents of the text field and also the number of columns used to display the text. Whenever new text is entered into the field the program receives key press and key release events that may be processed by overriding the `keyDown()` or `keyUp()` functions. Alternatively the text field generates an action event whenever the return key is pressed and passes the current contents of the text field to the `action()` function as a `String` parameter — the return character is not appended to the string. For password applications the `setEchoCharacter()`, `getEchoChar()` and `echoCharIsSet()` functions may be used to ensure that an echo character will replace any other characters typed in the text field. A `TextArea` constructor can specify the initial contents of the text area and also the number of rows and columns used to display the text — the `getRows()` and `getColumns()` functions return the actual size of the text area. The `TextArea` class `appendText()`, `insertText()` and `replaceText()` functions allow the text to be modified by the program — the user can only change the text if the text area is set as modifiable.

The `Button` class represents a basic button component — pressing the button sends an action event by calling the `action()` function with the button object as the `target` field of the `Event` parameter and the button's string label as the `Object` parameter. The contents of a button's label can be managed using the `Button` class `setLabel()` and `getLabel()` functions. The `Checkbox` class is similar to the `Button` class but the button is associated with a check mark that is automatically flipped on and off whenever the button is pressed. As for the `Button` class, an action event is sent every time that the button is pressed — however, in this case the second parameter to the `action()` function is a `Boolean` object that indicates whether the check mark is now on (`true`) or off (`false`). In addition to the `setLabel()` and `getLabel()` functions there are also `setState()` and `getState()` functions that can be called to directly manipulate the state of the check box. Furthermore, a check box can be associated with a `CheckboxGroup` object — at most one check box in a group can be set and if a second check box is turned on then the first check box is automatically turned off. The `CheckboxGroup` class provides `setCurrent()` and `getCurrent()` functions to manage the currently active check box in the group.

The Scrollbar class represents a scrollbar component with a slider bubble than can be moved from one end of the bar to the other — there are two orientations of scrollbar and these can be selected by passing the HORIZONTAL or VERTICAL constants to the constructor. Moving the scrollbar bubble directly generates a SCROLL_ABSOLUTE event whose arg field references an Integer object containing the new bubble position — alternatively, pressing one of the line gadgets sends a SCROLL_LINE_DOWN or SCROLL_LINE_UP event and pressing the page gadgets sends SCROLL_PAGE_DOWN or SCROLL_PAGE_UP events. The setValue() and getValue() functions manipulate the value held by the scrollbar and the getMinimum() and getMaximum() functions return the range of permissible values. The scrollbar's line increment value is controlled by the setLineIncrement() and getLineIncrement() functions whilst the functions setPageIncrement() and getPageIncrement() work with the page increment value instead.

The Choice class represents a popup list from which an item can be selected — clicking on the choice component causes the list to pop up and choosing an item invokes the action() function passing the string of the selected item as the second parameter. The Choice class constructor sets up a choice component with an empty list — the addItem() function allows the list to be filled in and the countItems() function returns the number of items in the list. The select() function sets the selected item programmatically whilst the getSelectedItem(), getSelectedIndex() and getItem() (from index) functions are used to retrieve the current selection — the selected item is displayed when the list is not in the popup state. An alternative to the Choice class is provided by the List class — this defines equivalents of all the Choice class functions and also allows multiple items to be selected. There are `addItem()`, `replaceItem()`, `delItem()`, `delItems()` and `clear()` functions for controlling the set of available list entries. The functions `select()` and `deselect()` allow individual items to be selected or deselected and the `isSelected()` function returns `true` if a particular item is selected. The `setMultipleSelections()` function determines whether multiple selections from the list are possible and the `allowsMultipleSelections()` function tests if this option is set or not — lists that allow only a single selection automatically deselect the previously selected item if another item is selected. The `getSelectedItems()` and `getSelectedIndexes()` functions provide alternatives to the `getSelectedItem()`, `getSelectedIndex()` and `getItem()` functions whenever multiple selections are enabled. A `List` object sends `LIST_SELECT` and `LIST_DESELECT` events when the user respectively selects or deselects an item by clicking on it — the `arg` field of the event is an `Integer` object that indicates which item in the list was selected. Alternatively, double clicking a list item sends an action event that includes a `String` object containing the label of the item. Finally, the `List` component constructor can accept a parameter to specify how many items to display in the list's scroll box — the `makeVisible()` function is called to force the list to display a particular item within this box.

13.4 Container Classes

The `Container` class extends the `Component` class and provides the additional functionality necessary for a component to contain sub-components — in particular, the `add()` function allows new components to be added to a container. For example, a frame window object can display a two-by-two grid of components — this grid is filled with four buttons using the frame's `add()` function:

```
import java.awt.*;

public class Application {
  public static void main(String[] params)
      throws InterruptedException {
    Frame frame = new MyFrame();
    GridLayout manager =
          new GridLayout(2,2);
    frame.resize(300,300);
    frame.setLayout(manager);
    frame.add(new Button("Top Left"));
    frame.add(new Button("Top Right"));
    frame.add(new Button("Bottom Left"));
    frame.add(new Button("Bottom Right"));
    frame.show();
    synchronized (frame) {
      frame.wait();
    }
    frame.dispose();
  }
}
```

The choice of layout for the components within a container is usually determined by a layout manager from a class such as `GridLayout` — the next section looks in more detail at the various layout manager classes but note here that a container's layout manager is manipulated using the `Container` class `setLayout()` and `getLayout()` functions. A window's `show()` function must be called to make the window visible — the `dispose()` function destroys the window and releases any resources it was using. Here the `Object` class `wait()` function waits until the `MyFrame` class signals that the user has requested closure of the window — the `Frame` class `dispose()` function is then called to destroy the window. A common alternative is simply to call the `System` class `exit()` function directly from the `MyFrame` class.

In addition to the `add()` function, the `Container` class also defines remove() and removeAll() functions for removing various components from a container. The countComponents() function returns the current number of components in a container whilst the getComponent() and getComponents() functions retrieve references to one or more of the contained components. Alternatively, the locate() function will determine which component within a container actually holds a particular point — the function returns the container itself if the point lies outside all contained components but is still within the container and it returns null if the point is outside the container. The inherited Component class function inside() is used to test whether the point lies within a particular component. Finally, the insets() function returns an Insets object that describes the extent of any borders around the edges of the container — for example, the Frame class has an inset at the top to hold its title bar and insets around the other three edges for the window frame.

The Panel class is the simplest container class — it just implements all the functions of the abstract Container class and so allows a series of components to be grouped within it. The Applet class described in the next chapter is derived from the Panel class — by default both the Panel class and its Applet subclass use the layout manager provided by the FlowLayout class.

The Window class is another container class — Window objects represent top-level windows without a title bar or border. The Window class constructor expects a reference to a Frame object that is associated with the parent of the new window — as noted in section 13.1 any events not processed directly by the window are passed along to its parent. In addition to any unhandled events from its contained components, a window may also receive a number of events specific to windows. A window receives a WINDOW_EXPOSE event when it becomes visible, a WINDOW_MOVED event when its position has changed and a WINDOW_DESTROY event when the user closes the window

— it may also receive `WINDOW_ICONIFY` and `WINDOW_DEICONIFY` events if the underlying operating system allows the user to minimize and restore windows. A window is initially hidden and must be made visible with a call to the `show()` function — the `toFront()` and `toBack()` functions respectively send a window to the front or the back of the display order. The default layout manager for a window is provided by the `BorderLayout` class — the `Window` class `pack()` function may be called to lay out the window as neatly as possible after taking into account the preferred sizes of its contained components. Whenever a window is no longer required it can be destroyed by calling the `dispose()` function and this action also releases all of the system resources that were allocated to the window. Finally, the `getWarningString()` function returns the string that will be displayed in any window that is considered 'insecure' — this usually applies to applets running under a Web browser and indeed the warning string is defined by the `"awt.appletWarning"` system property or alternatively defaults to the `"Warning: Applet Window"` string.

The `Frame` class is a subclass of the `Window` class that is used to represent top-level windows with a title bar and a border — the `Frame` class also implements the `MenuContainer` interface discussed in section 13.6 and so it can support a window which has a menu bar. A title string may be passed to a `Frame` object constructor or alternatively the frame window can remain untitled — the `setTitle()` and `getTitle()` functions are also available to control the window title. The `setResizable()` and `isResizable()` functions determine if the user is allowed to resize the window or not. A menu bar can be added to the frame window using the `setMenuBar()` function and removed with the `remove()` function — the current menu bar is returned by the `getMenuBar()` function. The `Frame` class overrides the `dispose()` function to release any menu resources used by a frame window. For operating systems that support window icons the `setIconImage()`

and `getIconImage()` functions are provided for manipulating the icon's `Image` object. Finally, a frame window can set the cursor associated with it using the `setCursor()` function — the `getCursorType()` function returns the current type of cursor assigned. The various cursor types include `DEFAULT_CURSOR` (typically an arrow pointer), `CROSSHAIR_CURSOR` and `HAND_CURSOR` — there is also a `WAIT_CURSOR` type (usually an hour-glass) for indicating a lengthy processing activity, a `TEXT_CURSOR` type for text entry, a `MOVE_CURSOR` type used when re-positioning a window and a range of resizing cursor types (such as `S_RESIZE_CURSOR` or `NW_RESIZE_CURSOR`) that are displayed whilst the window is being resized in various compass directions.

13.5 Layout Managers

A container typically arranges its components using a layout manager — the container sets and retrieves its layout manager with the `Container` class `setLayout()` and `getLayout()` functions. All layout manager classes implement the `LayoutManager` interface — the functions in this interface are usually called automatically by the corresponding `Container` class functions such as `add()`, `remove()`, `removeAll()` and `layout()`.

One of the simplest layout manager classes is `BorderLayout` — this class provides the default layout manager for all `Window` and `Frame` objects. The `BorderLayout` manager handles five components that must be called `"North"`, `"South"`, `"East"`, `"West"` and `"Center"` — the `"North"` and `"South"` components are stretched horizontally across the top and bottom of the container, then the `"East"` and `"West"` components are stretched vertically to fill the gaps at the left and right of the container and finally the `"Center"` component is stretched to fill any remaining space in the middle of the container. The constructor can be passed parameters to specify horizontal and vertical gaps between the various components.

The `FlowLayout` class is the default for the `Panel` and `Applet` containers. This layout manager displays components at their preferred sizes and arranges them from left to right in a series of rows ordered from top to bottom. By default each row is centred horizontally within the container and there are gaps around the components five pixels wide — the `FlowLayout` constructor can be passed parameters to alter the horizontal and vertical gap sizes and to set the component row alignment to `CENTER`, `LEFT` or `RIGHT`.

The `CardLayout` class provides a layout manager that displays one contained component at a time — the individual components can be selected in series like flipping through a pack of cards. The `first()` and `last()` functions respectively flip to the first and last components added to the container — the `next()` and `previous()` functions move circularly through the list of components. Alternatively the `show()` function can be passed a string label parameter to bring a specific component into view.

The `GridLayout` class is used to lay out a series of components in a 2-dimensional grid of cells — all the cells are the same size with one component appearing in each cell. The number of rows and columns are specified as parameters to the layout manager constructor — gaps around the cells can also be set in this way. The `GridBagLayout` class is a somewhat more sophisticated variation on the grid layout theme — each component is associated with a `GridBagConstraints` object that controls how the manager can lay out the components in the container's grid. The `GridBagLayout` class functions `setConstraints()` and `getConstraints()` are used to manipulate the `GridBagConstraints` objects assigned to the various components. The constraints can instruct the layout manager to stetch the component to fill its display area or to anchor the unstretched component in the middle of this area, or at a particular edge or in a certain corner — the display area for a single component can consist of several different cells. It is also possible to specify how the rows and columns in the grid should be spaced and how much padding is placed around a component. The `GridBagConstraints` class `fill` field takes one of the values `NONE` (default), `HORIZONTAL`, `VERTICAL` or `BOTH` to indicate how to stretch a component. The `anchor` field is used to set the position of a component if it does not fill its display area — the `CENTER` (default) value puts the component in the middle of the display area, the values `NORTH`, `EAST`, `WEST` and `SOUTH` anchor the component at one edge and finally the values `NORTHEAST`, `NORTHWEST`, `SOUTHEAST` and `SOUTHWEST` place the component in a corner. The `gridx` and `gridy` fields specify the cell coordinates at the top-left corner of the component — the default value of `RELATIVE` places the components according to the order that they are added to the container. The `gridwidth` and `gridheight` fields determine the number of cells to assign to the component's display area — a value of `REMAINDER` indicates that the component is the last one in its row or column. The `weightx` and `weighty` fields are used to assign any spare vertical or horizontal space within the container to the rows and columns containing the component involved — the `insets`, `ipadx` and `ipady` fields can be used to pad individual components. The `GridBagConstraints` constructor provides an object with all fields set to their default values — individual fields need to be modified to the desired values before the `setConstraints()` function is called to associate a component with its constraints.

13.6 Menus and Dialogs

The menu and dialog components provide standardized ways of communicating with the user — a menu bar can be attached to a frame window and dialog boxes are popup windows that have a frame window as their parent. The menu component classes are not derived from the `Component` class but instead are subclasses of the `MenuComponent` class — the `Dialog` class is subclass of the `Window` class and the `FileDialog` class is derived from the Dialog class.

The MenuComponent class is the abstract superclass of all menu component classes — there is also a MenuContainer interface which is implemented by the Frame class. Menu components are arranged into a tree hierarchy with a MenuBar object at the root — the menu bar can contain a number of menus and each of these menus can hold menu items or sub-menus. The MenuComponent class getParent() function returns the menu component containing the current component — the MenuBar object returns null. The MenuComponent class also provides setFont() and getFont() functions to manage the font for a particular menu component — when a font is set, the same font is also used as the default for all sub-components.

The MenuBar class has add() and remove() functions to control which menus a menu bar contains — the getMenu() function retrieves a particular menu and the countMenus() functions indicates the number of menus currently in use. The functions setHelpMenu() and getHelpMenu() may be useful if the menu bar has a help menu. Similarly, the Menu class has add() and remove() functions to manipulate the items and sub-menus that it contains. The add() function can be passed a String object that is used to create a new menu item or alternatively a reference to a previously existing MenuItem object can be passed — the latter option is the only method applicable to sub-menus. A menu separator can be added using the addSeparator() function. The getItem() function returns a particular menu item and the countItems() function indicates the number of items in a menu. Some operating systems support 'tear-off' menus — this option is chosen by passing a flag to the Menu constructor. The Menu class isTearOff() function tests whether or not a particular menu can be torn off.

The MenuItem class is derived from the MenuComponent

class — it has the Menu class and the CheckboxMenuItem class as subclasses. A menu item sends an action event whenever it is selected — however, no event is generated when a menu is opened. The events are tyically handled by the frame window to which the menu belongs — the Event parameter to the action() function contains a reference to the menu item object and the Object parameter is a String object holding the associated label. For example:

```
public boolean action(Event e,Object info) {
  if (e.target instanceof MenuItem) {
    String s = (String)info;
    if (s.equals("Go")) {
      // perform processing
      return true;
    }
  }
  return false;
}
```

Here the code checks for an event from a menu item with the label "Go". A menu item can be passed its label as a constructor parameter and thereafter the label may be manipulated using the setLabel() and getLabel() functions — the label "-" is reserved for separator menu items. The enable(), disable() and isEnabled() functions determine whether the user can select a particular menu item — all menu items (except separators) are initially enabled. The CheckboxMenuItem class is very similar to the basic MenuItem class but it allows the user to flip a check mark on and off every time that its menu item is selected — the CheckboxMenuItem class defines getState() and setState() functions to manipulate the state of the check mark programmatically.

The Dialog class is subclass of Window and like the Frame class it represents a resizable window with a title bar and border — indeed it also defines setTitle() and getTitle() functions to process the title string as well as setResizable() and isResizable() functions to determine whether the user can resize the window or not. However, the `Dialog` constructor expects a reference to an object representing the frame window that acts as the popup window's parent — events are passed along to the parent if they are not handled directly by the dialog box. The constructor is also passed a flag to indicate whether the dialog box is 'modal' or not — a modal window prevents all other windows from receiving user input until it is dismissed. The `isModal()` function can be called to test whether a dialog box is modal or not.

The `FileDialog` class provides a specific implementation of a dialog box — it is used to allow the user to select the filename needed for loading or saving a file. The `FileDialog` constructor can be passed one of the constants `LOAD` or `SAVE` to select the type of dialog box required — by default the `LOAD` version is provided but in any case the `getMode()` function will return either `LOAD` or `SAVE` to indicate the actual mode type. The functions `setFile()` and `setDirectory()` are called to specify the default file and which directory contents to display. The `setFilenameFilter()` and `getFilenameFilter()` functions may be needed if a 'filename filter' is involved — the `FilenameFilter` interface `accept()` function allows the range of files displayed from a particular directory to be restricted. As with all windows, the dialog box is initially hidden and must be made visible with a call to the `show()` function — this function does not return until the user has selected a file. Finally, the `getDirectory()` and `getFile()` functions can be called to obtain the user's choices — the `getFile()` function returns a null `String` object if no file has been selected.

13.7 Images

The use of graphical images in Java is based around the `Image` class — each `Image` object represents a computerized image consisting of a rectangular grid of coloured dots called 'pixels'. There are two types of `Image` object — the first type obtains its image from an external source called an 'image producer' whilst the second acts as an off-screen drawable area. The first type of `Image` object is more common and is typically created using the `Applet` class `getImage()` function — alternative methods involve the `Toolkit` class version of this function or the `Component` class `createImage()` function that accepts an `ImageProducer` parameter. The second type of `Image` object is created by calling another version of the overloaded `Component` class `createImage()` function — this version accepts two integer parameters to fix the width and height of the off-screen image. In any case the `Image` object's image can be drawn using the `Graphics` class `drawImage()` function. The `Graphics` object involved is usually supplied to a window component's `paint()` function as its lone parameter — however, it is also possible to obtain a `Graphics` object for drawing to the off-screen image provided by the second type of `Image` object. The action of drawing an image with the `drawImage()` function may require that its pixels be obtained from the image producer — this can be a lengthy process and so it is run in the background with an 'image observer' receiving updates on progress through its `imageUpdate()` function. The `Component` version of the `imageUpdate()` function incrementally draws the image as more pixels become available. For example:

```
private Image image;

public MyComponent() {
  Toolkit toolkit = getToolkit();
  image = toolkit.getImage("image.gif");
}

public void paint(Graphics g) {
  g.drawImage(image,0,0,this);
}
```

The final parameter to the `drawImage()` function specifies that the component being painted will act as its own image observer — the incremental drawing operation occurs automatically whenever the inherited `imageUpdate()` function is called. However, it may be desirable to prepare an image for drawing in advance of calling the `drawImage()` function. This approach is possible using the `Component` class `prepareImage()` function — this returns `true` if the image is already available or alternatively starts to load the image and notifies an image observer of progress. If an image observer is not provided it is still possible to check the current status of the image loading process by calling the `Component` class `checkImage()` function. Both the `prepareImage()` and `checkImage()` functions can be used to load an image at its original size or alternatively scaled to fit a specific rectangular area.

The image observer mechanism is also used whenever the `Image` class functions `getWidth()`, `getHeight()` and `getProperty()` are called to obtain the size of an image and other properties associated with the image — if this information is not yet available then the functions return `-1` (or `null` for the `getProperty()` function) and an image observer is notified when the data is eventually determined. The `getProperty()` function accepts a `String` object as its first parameter and this is used to identify which property is required — for example, the `"comments"` property provides a string that contains a description of the image. As noted above the `getProperty()` function returns a null `Object` value if the image properties are not yet available but if a requested property does not actually exist then the `Image` class `UndefinedProperty` object is returned instead.

The `ImageObserver` interface defines only one function — the `imageUpdate()` function. This function provides notifications of the arrival of image pixels and the availability of image width, height and property information — it also reports error or abort conditions. The second parameter to the `imageUpdate()` function contains a series of flags that indicate the cause of the current update.

The SOMEBITS flag is set if new pixel bits for the image have arrived and the other function parameters specify which bits. The ALLBITS flag is set when all bits have been delivered — for multi-frame images the FRAMEBITS flag can be used to indicate the end of the current frame. The WIDTH, HEIGHT and PROPERTIES flags notify the observer that the relevant information about the image is available — the width and height values are supplied to the imageUpdate() function. Finally, the ABORT and ERROR flags are set whenever the image loading procedure has terminated abruptly — the ABORT flag indicates that this action was requested by the program.

The MediaTracker class provides a convenient way to prepare images prior to drawing — this is an alternative to using the Component class prepareImage() and checkImage() functions. The MediaTracker class currently works only with images but it will eventually also work with the AudioClip objects described in the next chapter. An image is loaded by passing it to the MediaTracker object's addImage() function (optionally specifying a new image size if scaling is required) and then calling one of the MediaTracker class functions waitForAll() or waitForID() — the ID value for a particular image is set by a parameter to the addImage() function and images with lower ID values are loaded first. Both the waitForAll() and waitForID() functions can also be set to time-out after so many milliseconds if the images are not yet ready — the checkAll() and checkID() functions can be called to determine when the images are eventually ready. Once loading is complete the MediaTracker class functions isErrorAny() or isErrorID() must be called to check whether the images have been successfully prepared — the functions getErrorsAny() and getErrorsID() return references to any Image objects for which an error was encountered. Another possibility is to call the statusAll() or statusID() functions to obtain the image status flags — there are LOADING, COMPLETE, ABORTED and ERRORED flags with a zero return value indicating that loading of an image has not yet begun.

13.8 Image Producers and Consumers

An object that can supply an image implements the `ImageProducer` interface — similarly, the interface `ImageConsumer` is implemented by any object that wants to use the image provided by an image producer. In particular, an `Image` object internally creates an image consumer to obtain an image from its producer — the image producer associated with an `Image` object can be obtained by calling its `getProducer()` function. Each image producer maintains a list of consumers that are interested in receiving its image data — the `ImageProducer` interface defines the `addConsumer()`, `removeConsumer()` and `isConsumer()` functions for managing this list. There is also a `startProduction()` function to tell the image producer to start sending the image to its consumers and a `requestTopDownLeftRightResend()` function that asks the producer to provide the image pixels in a standard order from left to right and from top to bottom.

An image producer sends information to an image consumer using the `ImageConsumer` interface that is implemented by the consumer object. The basic procedure involves calls to the following three functions:

1. `setHints()` advises the consumer of the image delivery format
2. `setPixels()` actually delivers the pixels to the consumer
3. `imageComplete()` notifies the consumer that all pixels have been sent

The `setHints()` function passes a collection of flags to allow the consumer to optimize its processing of the pixel data that it receives. For example, the `RANDOMPIXELORDER` flag indicates that the pixels may arrive in any order whereas the `TOPDOWNLEFTRIGHT` flag means that the pixels will be delivered left to right and top to bottom — the former option is the default if the `setHints()` function is never called. Furthermore, the `COMPLETESCANLINES` flag tells the consumer that the pixels will be sent in blocks that contain complete scanlines, the `SINGLEFRAME` flag means that the image has only one frame and does not, for example, represent a video sequence, and finally the `SINGLEPASS` flag indicates that the image will be defined in a single pass rather than requiring a series of passes each providing the same image but at progressively higher resolutions.

The `setPixels()` function may be called one or more times — the function receives `top`, `left`, `width` and `height` parameters to specify which pixels from the image are currently being delivered. The pixels arrive in a **`byte`** or **`int`** array and the colour information must be extracted using the `ColorModel` object also passed to the `setPixels()` function — the next section deals with pixel colours and colour models in more detail. The `imageComplete()` function is invoked after the final call to `setPixels()` — it passes the `STATICIMAGEDONE` flag to say that an image is complete and there are no more frames to follow or it passes the `SINGLEFRAMEDONE` flag to mark the end of one frame and the start of the next. If an error occurs whilst the image is being delivered or if the delivery process is deliberately aborted then the `imageComplete()` function respectively passes the `IMAGEERROR` or `IMAGEABORTED` flags.

Finally, the `ImageConsumer` interface also defines the functions `setDimensions()`, `setProperties()` and `setColorModel()`. The `setDimensions()` functions passes the width and height of the image and the `setProperties()` function adds properties to the image that can be retrieved using the `Image` class `getProperty()` function described in the previous section. The `setColorModel()` function is called to allow the image consumer to optimize its processing — the function supplies the colour model that will be used in most of the calls to the `setPixels()` function.

The `MemoryImageSource` class is a standard Java class from the `java.awt.image` package that implements the `ImageProducer` interface — the class allows an image to be constructed from an array of pixel data held in memory. The `MemoryImageSource` constructor is passed the width and height of the image as well as an **`int`** or **`byte`** array containing the actual image information. The constructor also requires a `ColorModel` object that is used to extract the colour information from the pixels — by default the colour model returned by the `ColorModel` class `getRGBdefault()` function is used. Finally, the properties associated with the image can be set by passing them as an optional `Hashtable` parameter to the constructor of the `MemoryImageSource` object.

The `PixelGrabber` class is also defined in the `java.awt.image` package. This class implements the `ImageConsumer` interface and it allows selected pixels from an image to be grabbed — the pixels are stored in an **`int`** array using the format defined by the default `RGB` colour model. The `PixelGrabber` constructor is passed parameters to specify the rectangular image area of interest and the `Image` object or `ImageProducer` interface to be used in retrieving the pixels — the constructor is also passed the array in which to place the grabbed pixels. To actually grab the pixels the `grabPixels()` function must be called — a parameter can be specified that causes the pixel grabbing procedure to timeout after so many milliseconds. Finally, the `status()` function may be called to determine the status of the image involved — this function returns the same flags as passed to the `updateImage()` function of an image observer.

13.9 Colours

The `java.awt` package defines the `Color` class to allow colours to be specified in a standardized way. The

Color class works principally with colours split into their three colour components red, green and blue — the component values range from 0 (no contribution) up to 255 (maximum contribution). A new Color object can be constructed by passing it an RGB triple of **int** colour component values — the individual components can be retrieved using the getRed(), getGreen() and getBlue() functions. Alternatively, the three components can be packed into a single **int** quantity using bits 16 to 23 for the red component, bits 8 to 15 for the blue component and bits 0 to 7 for the green component — the getRGB() function returns colour values in this format. The Color class also pre-defines a series of Color objects such as white, black, yellow, green, blue and red that represent the corresponding colours — the brighter() and darker() functions can be used to create lighter or darker shades of a particular colour. There is also a static getColor() function which retrieves colours from the system properties list and a few other functions that convert between RGB and HSB (hue-saturation-brightness) colour formats.

Java uses colour models to convert between pixel values and the corresponding colours — all colour model classes are derived from the abstract ColorModel superclass defined in the java.awt.image package. The ColorModel constructor accepts the number of bits per pixel used by the colour model — this value is stored in the pixel_bits field and returned by the getPixelSize() function. The getRed(), getGreen() and getBlue() functions convert pixel values to colour components normalized in the range 0 to 255 — there is also a getAlpha() function which provides the transparency value for a pixel again in the range 0 (transparent) to 255 (opaque). Alternatively, the getRGB() function returns the colour components packed into an **int** value much as the Color class getRGB() function does — however, the transparency value appears as bits 24 to 31. Finally, the static function getRGBdefault() returns the default RGB colour model. This colour model uses a pixel format involving one 32-bit integer per pixel coded in the same manner as the values returned by the `ColorModel` class `getRGB()` function — in other words, the `getRGB()` function performs an identity transformation when the default `RGB` colour model is in force.

The `ColorModel` class has two standard subclasses both defined in the `java.awt.image` package — the `DirectColorModel` class takes the colour information directly from the pixel bits whilst the `IndexColorModel` class uses the pixel values to extract colour information from a separate colour table. In addition to the number of bits per pixel the `DirectColorModel` constructor is passed bit masks to specify which pixel bits correspond to the `RGB` colour components and to the transparency value — the bits assigned to each field must be contiguous. The `getRedMask()`, `getGreenMask()`, `getBlueMask()` and `getAlphaMask()` functions return these bit mask values — the actual component values for a particular pixel are returned by `DirectColorModel` class versions of the `getRed()`, `getGreen()`, `getBlue()` and `getAlpha()` functions (or alternatively in packed-form by the `getRGB()` function).

The `IndexColorModel` class takes colour components from entries in a 'colour table' (or colour map) — the colour table is passed to the `IndexColorModel` constructor as separate arrays for red, green, blue and (optionally) transparency values or alternatively as a single array with all values for each entry being packed together as a sequence of three or four bytes. The constructor specifies the number of bits per pixel and the size of the colour table as individual parameters — any pixel values corresponding to entries beyond the end of the table are assigned the colour black. All the entries in the colour table can be retrieved using the functions `getReds()`, `getGreens()`, `getBlues()` and `getAlphas()` — the size of the colour table is returned by the `getMapSize()` function. The entry for an individual pixel is available from the `IndexColorModel` class versions of the `getRed()`, `getGreen()`, `getBlue()` and `getAlpha()` functions — the `getRGB()` function supplies this information in the standard packed format. Finally, the `IndexColorModel` constructor can optionally be passed a transparent pixel value — pixels with this value are transparent regardless of their colour table entry. The `getTransparentPixel()` function returns the transparent pixel value if it is defined and returns `-1` otherwise.

13.10 Image Filters

The `FilteredImageSource` and `ImageFilter` classes are defined by the `java.awt.image` package to support filtering of images. An image filter intercepts the image data as it flows from an image producer to an image consumer and modifies it in some way — the standard Java classes `CropImageFilter` and `RGBImageFilter` are derived from `ImageFilter` and respectively crop an image to a reduced size or alter the RGB colours of the image pixels.

The `FilteredImageSource` class implements the `ImageProducer` interface and the `ImageFilter` class implements the `ImageConsumer` interface. The following figure illustrates the flow of information used to filter an image:

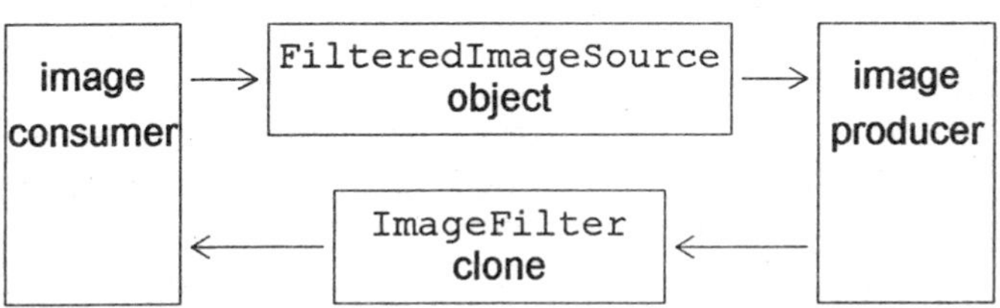

The `FilteredImageSource` object acts as a new image producer — its constructor is passed references to an existing image producer and an `ImageFilter` object and it uses these to implement the required functionality. When an image consumer needs the filtered image it sends requests to the `FilteredImageSource` object and these are forwarded to the existing image producer — however, this producer actually supplies data to a clone of the original `ImageFilter` object and the clone passes the data along to the ultimate consumer but only after filtering it first.

An `ImageFilter` object acts as a 'null filter' and simply transfers the image data to the consumer unaltered. User-defined subclasses of the `ImageFilter` class can implement the desired filtering action — in particular, the abstract Java class `RGBImageFilter` can be subclassed simply by providing an implementation of the `filterRGB()` function. Alternatively, the standard Java class `CropImageFilter` may be used directly to reduce the size of an image — the `CropImageFilter` constructor is passed `top`, `left`, `width` and `height` parameters that define a 'crop rectangle' which fixes the new outline of the filtered image. This class basically sends the image data to the consumer untouched but the parameters to the functions `setPixels()`, `setDimensions()` and `setProperties()` are slightly modified before the consumer versions of these functions are invoked. The `setPixels()` function checks that at least some of the pixels supplied actually appear within the crop rectangle or else it does not forward the data — if some pixels are indeed visible then the parameters are modified by translating the origin to the top-left corner of the cropped image and intersecting the bounding rectangle of the delivered pixels with the crop rectangle. The `CropImageFilter` version of the `setDimensions()` function ignores its parameters and instead sends the consumer the values supplied to the `CropImageFilter` constructor. Finally, the `setProperties()` function adds the `"croprect"` property to the image's property list using the value `new Rectangle(top,left,width,height)`.

The `RGBImageFilter` class is an abstract utility class which can be subclassed to provide image filters that modify the colours of various pixels within an image — these subclasses must implement the `filterRGB()` function. This function supplies the pixels from the original image one by one using the default `RGB` colour model and specifying the coordinates of each pixel — the function must return the corresponding filtered pixels using the same colour model. In the basic mode of operation the `setPixels()` function filters each pixel through the `filterRGB()` function before sending them on to the consumer — the `setPixels()` function filters the pixels by converting them to the default `RGB` colour model format and passing them to the `filterRGBPixels()` function. However, if a user-defined subclass sets the protected `canFilterIndexColorModel` field to `true` then a more efficient mode is possible if the image is delivered using an `IndexColorModel` colour model. In this case the `setColorModel()` function is able to pass the colour table entries through the `filterRGB()` function instead of filtering every pixel separately — a subclass should only enable this mode if the filtering process depends only on individual pixel values and is independent of pixel coordinates. The `setColorModel()` function actually filters the colour table by passing its colour model parameter to the `filterIndexColorModel()` function — this calls the `filterRGB()` function for each colour table entry using `-1` for the pixel coordinates and eventually returns a new colour model object representing the filtered pixel values. The `setColorModel()` function then calls the `substituteColorModel()` function to save the original and filtered colour models in the protected `origmodel` and `newmodel` fields. The new colour model is passed to the consumer's `setColorModel()` function instead of the original. Now whenever the `setPixels()` function is invoked it checks to see if the current colour model matches the `origmodel` field and if it does then the colour model from the `newmodel` field can be substituted and no other processing is necessary.

13.11 Summary

Java informs a window-based application of user input by sending `Event` objects to various window components — the type of event is identified by the `id` field of the `Event` object and the component to which the event is originally delivered appears in the `target` field. Many common events are passed to specialized functions such as `action()`, `mouseMove()` or `keyUp()` — less common events are handled directly by the general `handleEvent()` function. To create new window components with user-defined behaviour the standard Java classes must be subclassed and the event handling functions overridden — these functions should return `true` if they handle a particular event and `false` if the event is to be passed to the component's container or parent instead. Most standard window component classes are derived from the `Component` class — the `Canvas` class allows an application to draw directly on the screen, the `Label` class provides fixed text fields whilst the `TextField` and `TextArea` classes support user-editable text, the `Button` class represents push buttons, the `Checkbox` class allows a check mark to be flipped on or off and the `CheckboxGroup` class prevents setting of multiple checks in the same group, the `Scrollbar` class provides vertical or horizontal scrollbars, and finally the `Choice` and `List` classes permit the user to select items from a list. Several components can be arranged within a container — the `Container` class is derived from the `Component` class and is the abstract superclass of the other container classes. The `Panel` class is the most basic container and simply allows components to be grouped together — the `Applet` class is an important subclass of the `Panel` class. The `Window` class is another container class that provides top-level windows without any decoration — the `Frame` class is a subclass representing windows with a title bar and border that can define their own cursor style and have a menu bar attached. Menus and menu items are arranged in a tree hierarchy with a `MenuBar` object at the root of the tree — the `Menu` class represents menus whilst the classes `MenuItem` and `CheckboxMenuItem` represent menu items. The `Window` class is also the superclass of the `Dialog` class and this has the `FileDialog` class as a subclass — the `Dialog` class provides general purpose dialog boxes whilst the `FileDialog` class allows the user to select a file for loading or saving. The components within a container are typically laid out using a layout manager — a layout manager is an object that implements the `LayoutManager` interface and it is associated with a container using the `Container` class `setLayout()` function. The `BorderLayout` manager is the default for windows — it manages five components called `"North"`, `"South"`, `"East"`, `"West"` and `"Center"`. The `FlowLayout` manager is the default for panels and applets — it arranges components in rows from left to right and from top to bottom. The `CardLayout` manager allows a series of components to be displayed one at a time. The `GridLayout` manager places its components in a grid of rectangular cells and the `GridBagLayout` manager does likewise but together with the assistance of the `GridBagConstraints` class it permits a somewhat more sophisticated arrangement. Java calls a component's `paint()` function whenever it needs to be drawn. A program can request that a particular component be updated by calling its `repaint()` function — as soon as possible after this Java calls the component's `update()` function and this clears the current contents before invoking the `paint()` function. A `Graphics` object is passed to both the `update()` and `paint()` calls and this object provides a variety of functions for re-drawing the component. Java provides a range of other classes for working with text, colours and images. The `Font` class represents individual fonts whilst the `FontMetrics` class provides information on character dimensions such as the width (in pixels) of a text string. The `Color` class allows colours to be represented in a standardized manner and a colour model class is used to determine which colours to use for various pixel values — with the `DirectColorModel` class the colours are encoded directly within the pixel bits but with the `IndexColorModel` class the pixels values are used to select colours from a separate colour table. The use of images in Java is based on the `Image` class — an `Image` object is typically created using the `Applet` class `getImage()` function or the `Component` class `createImage()` function. An image may be drawn by calling the `Graphics` class `drawImage()` function. If all the pixels for the image are not yet available then the `updateImage()` function of the associated image observer will be called as more image data is received — the `Component` class version of this function draws the image incrementally. Alternatively, the image can be prepared before it is drawn — the `MediaTracker` class provides a convenient way of pre-loading the image pixels. Images are supplied by image producers and are used by image consumers — these objects respectively implement the `ImageProducer` and `ImageConsumer` interfaces. An image is transferred whenever a consumer requests that its producer deliver the pixels — the transfer is achieved through a series of calls to the `ImageConsumer` interface `setPixels()` function. The `MemoryImageSource` class provides image producers that generate images from an array of pixels stored in memory — conversely, the `PixelGrabber` class allows pixels from an image to be grabbed and placed into an array. As an image is sent from producer to consumer it can be intercepted by an image filter that modifies the image in some way — Java provides the `FilteredImageSource` and `ImageFilter` classes to implement image filters. The `CropImageFilter` class allows an image to be cropped to a smaller size. Finally, the `RGBImageFilter` class is an abstract utility superclass that permits subclasses to alter the pixel colour information in an image simply by implementing the `filterRGB()` function.

14. Applets

One of the most popular uses of Java is to develop mini applications (applets) that can be run by a World Wide Web browser — the `java.applet` package provides the `Applet` class to handle this scenario. The Web consists of a collection of interconnected Web pages into which various forms of active content such as applets can be embedded — the `HTML` formatting language is used to specify the 'hyperlinks' from one document to another and also to embed an applet within a page. An applet is created by defining a subclass of the `Applet` class and overriding the appropriate functions to make the applet perform as required — the Web browser communicates with the applet by calling various `Applet` class functions and the applet can interact with its environment by making requests to the browser. In particular, the applet can pass message strings to the browser that should be displayed in its status bar or alternatively it can ask the browser to show a new Web page. The `Applet` class also provides functions that make handling images and audio clips relatively easy — the `URL` (Uniform Resource Locator) class from the `java.net` package is available for locating more general resources. The `java.net` package also provides several functions to support low-level Internet communications — both datagram and stream protocols are available. This functionality is useful when creating a server application to which a collection of client applets will connect.

14.1 Web Pages

The World Wide Web is a global collection of computer documents interconnected by 'hyperlinks' — moving from one document to another just requires a click of the mouse button. These 'Web pages' are basically static but they can be enlivened in various ways by the addition of active content — in particular, a Java applet can be embedded within a Web page.

The layout of a Web page is typically described using `HTML`

(HyperText Markup Language) — this language provides a straightforward mechanism for creating hot-spots within a document that act as hyperlinks to other documents. The fundamental units in HTML are 'elements' — each element consists of start and end tags enclosing some text. The tags describe the type of element involved and are enclosed within angle brackets < > — the end tag has the character '/' immediately before the tag name. For example, the following element formats the enclosed text using a bold font:

```
<B>Here is some bold text.</B>
```

The tag names are case-insensitive but they are conventionally written in upper case.

Elements can be nested one within another — the HTML element typically encompasses all other elements. Within the HTML element there are HEAD and BODY elements — the HEAD element provides the header for the document and the BODY element contains the actual content of the document. The TITLE element is placed in the document header — it defines a title string for the document that is used in a Web browser's title bar. A hyperlink can be defined within the BODY element using the A (anchor) element — the start tag of this element contains the HREF attribute that determines the destination of the hyperlink. The destination is specified as a URL (Uniform Resource Locator) — for example:

```
<HTML>
<HEAD><TITLE>Introduction</TITLE></HEAD>
<BODY>
      .
      .
<A HREF="http://www.megacorp.com/demo.html">
  Click here for demo!</A>
      .
      .
</BODY>
</HTML>
```

Here clicking on the hot-stop causes the browser to jump to the demo.html document provided by the Web site www.megacorp.com — section 14.4 covers URL usage in more detail.

The APPLET element is used to embed an applet within a document. The CODE attribute determines which applet is involved and the amount of space required by the applet within the document may be specified using the WIDTH and HEIGHT attributes — for example:

```
<APPLET CODE=Test WIDTH=100 HEIGHT=100>
<PARAM NAME="x" VALUE="0">
<PARAM NAME="y" VALUE="0">
</APPLET>
```

Here the Test applet is run — the PARAM elements are used to provide the applet with default parameter values via the Applet class getParameter() function. The next section describes the process of actually running an applet whilst section 14.3 looks at applet parameters and other aspects of the applet environment.

14.2 Applets Alive

An applet is a mini-application defined as a subclass of the standard Applet class from the java.applet package — the Applet class extends the Panel class and so it can act as a container for other window components. The most important Applet class functions are probably the init(), start(), stop() and destroy() functions — the basic versions perform no action and they must be overridden in the derived applet class. When the Web page containing the applet is visited for the first time, the CODE attribute of the APPLET element provides the name of the applet class — a new object of this class is created and its init() function is invoked. The start() function is then called and the applet becomes active. If the Web browser moves to another part of the Web page (or to a entirely new document) and so hides the applet then the applet's stop() function is called and it becomes inactive — the applet is reactivated and its `start()` function is re-invoked every time that its part of the Web page is revisited. The `Applet` class `isActive()` function returns `true` whenever the applet is active. Eventually the applet will be discarded and then its `stop()` function is called a final time, the `destroy()` function is executed and the applet is destroyed. The `init()` and `destroy()` functions are used to allocate and release any resources such as additional threads which the applet needs — the `start()` and `stop()` functions are typically used to turn on and off effects such as animation that are unnecessary whenever the applet is not visible.

A simple example of an applet is provided by the `Beeper` class:

```
import java.applet.*;
import java.awt.*;

class Beeper extends Applet {
  public void init() {
    add(new Button("Press Me"));
  }

  public boolean action(Event e,Object x) {
    if (e.target instanceof Button) {
      play(getCodeBase(),"audio/beep.au");
      return true;
    }
    return false;
  }
}
```

This applet displays a single button with the label `"Press Me"` — the position of the button is determined by the default `FlowLayout` manager. When the button is pressed the applet receives an action event that specifies the `Button` object as its target — the `action()` function plays an audio clip stored in the `beep.au` file within the applet sub-directory `audio`. The next section discusses the `getCodeBase()` function used for finding the applet directory and section 14.4 covers audio clips in much more detail.

The `WIDTH` and `HEIGHT` attributes of the `APPLET` element indicate the initial size of the applet within the Web page. The applet can request that the browser modify its size by calling the `Applet` class `resize()` function but the request may be ignored — the `size()` function inherited from the `Component` class returns the current size of the applet.

14.3 The Applet Environment

The `Applet` class provides several functions for interacting with its environment — for example, the `showStatus()` function requests that its `String` parameter be displayed in the browser's status bar. There is also a `getParameter()` function that is used to read in parameters set in the Web page using `PARAMETER` elements nested within the `APPLET` element — section 14.1 provides an example of the text needed within an `HTML` file to define an applet parameter. Both the `NAME` and `VALUE` attributes of the `PARAMETER` element must be strings — the `NAME` attribute names the individual parameter and is passed to the `getParameter()` function whereas the `VALUE` attribute is supplied as the return value of this function. This mechanism provides an easy way to modify the behaviour of an applet without recompiling any code. The `getParameterInfo()` function returns an array of elements that describe the meaning of the various parameters — each element is in fact an array of three `String` objects, the first containing the name of the parameter, the second specifying the type of the parameter and the last giving information about the use of the parameter. The `Applet` class version of the function `getParameterInfo()` simply returns `null` and a derived applet class should override the function to provide a description of the parameters which it understands. Similarly, the `Applet` class `getAppletInfo()` function also returns `null` and each applet class can override this function to return information about itself.

The getCodeBase() function returns the directory containing the applet using URL format whilst the getDocumentBase() function returns the URL of the document that contains the applet. The former URL is typically used to find images and audio clips needed by the applet — the previous section provided one example of this usage and the next section examines the whole subject in more detail. The Applet class also defines a getAppletContext() function — this returns a reference to an AppletContext interface which can be used to interact with the applet's document and the Web browser. The AppletContext interface getApplet() function returns a reference to another applet within the document — each applet is identified by a string name set using the NAME attribute of the corresponding APPLET element in the HTML file. Alternatively, the getApplets() function returns an Enumeration object that iterates through all the applets in the document. Finally, the AppletContext interface showDocument() function requests that the browser display a new Web page.

14.4 Multi-Media Resources

The Applet class also makes it easy to load images and audio clips — these are typically stored as .gif and .au files. An image can be obtained by calling the Applet class getImage() function and passing the URL for the image — it is common to store images associated with an applet in an images sub-directory of the applet directory and to use a relative URL to locate the image as follows:

```
public void init() {
    image = getImage(getCodeBase(),
                     "images/image.gif");
          .
          .
}
```

The image is drawn by calling the Graphics class drawImage() function — if necessary the image can be prepared beforehand using a MediaTracker object as discussed in section 13.7.

Similarly, section 14.2 illustrated how easy it is to play an audio clip using the Applet class play() function — alternatively, the getAudioClip() function returns an AudioClip interface reference. The AudioClip interface defines the three functions play(), loop() and stop() — the loop() function causes the audio clip to play repeatedly in a loop until the stop() function is called.

The locations of both images and audio clips are specified using the URL format — this format is embodied by the URL class from the java.net package. Each URL identifies a particular protocol type — for Web applications this is usually http (HyperText Transport Protocol). The URL also contains a host machine name such as www.megacorp.com and a resource name such as demo.html or audio/beep.au to identify the particular resource involved. Hence, the full URL for an audio clip looks something like the following:

```
http://www.megacorp.com/audio/beep.au
```

A URL object can be created by passing it a string in URL format — alternatively an existing URL can be modified with a relative part specified as a string in much the same way as for the Applet class getImage(), getAudioClip() and play() functions. The URL class functions getProtocol(), getHost() and getFile() may be used to extract the individual components of the URL. A URL object is typically used to create a URLConnection object that will actually connect to the resource identified by the URL. This resource can be practically anything and need not be just an image or an audio clip. Many resources are supplied using MIME format — this allows an object to be serialized for transmission to a new destination and then to be reconstructed on arrival. The URL class provides the openConnection() function to create a URLConnection object — the getContent() function of this object can then be called to transfer an object from the resource. The URL class getContent() function is equivalent to openConnection().getContent() — the URL connection is made and an object is transferred. An alternative procedure uses the URL class function openStream() to obtain an InputStream object which can read directly from the resource — a URLConnection object is created internally and its getInputStream() function is invoked to actually create the stream.

14.5 Internet Communications

The Java language is closely linked with the Internet in the form of the World Wide Web — the URL format enables resources to be located in a reasonably straightforward manner. However, the java.net package also provides classes for low-level network communications and these can be useful when setting up a Java server to which a collection of client applets all connect. The security features of Java usually prevent an applet from connecting to any machine except the one providing the applet — this means that two applets cannot connect directly but must pass messages via the server machine. A full blown Java application runs on the server to handle the flow of messages — the actions of the various applets are coordinated by the server application. The following figure illustrates the situation:

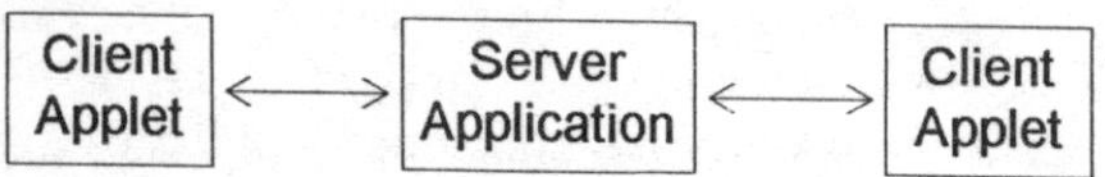

Every machine (or 'host') connected to the Internet is assigned an IP (Internet Protocol) address that uniquely identifies it — the standard Java class InetAddress is defined to encapsulate an IP address. The static functions getLocalHost() and getByName() respectively return InetAddress objects for the local machine and for a host with a particular name — the getHostName() function converts back to a host name and the getAddress()

function returns the raw `IP` address as an array of four bytes. A communications channel to a particular machine is further identified by a port number — messages from a variety of sources can arrive at a single port but an individual channel is uniquely specified by the following five items:

1. the protocol involved
2. the source host
3. the source port
4. the destination host
5. the destination port

The are two low-level protocols supported by the `java.net` package — the first uses the `DatagramPacket` and `DatagramSocket` classes whilst the second uses the `ServerSocket` and `Socket` classes. A 'socket' represents one end of a communications channel and messages are sent from one socket to another as a series of 'packets'. The 'datagram protocol' simply sends off packets and hopes that they arrive safely — the other protocol is a 'stream protocol' and this establishes a 'connection' over the communications channel which ensures that the packets are not lost, duplicated or received out of sequence.

The `DatagramPacket` class has a pair of constructors for creating two distinct sorts of object — one sort is used for receiving packets whilst the other is used for sending packets. Both constructors supply a **`byte`** buffer to hold the packet's data — for outgoing packets the constructor also specifies the destination host and port number. The `getData()` function can be used to examine the contents of a packet and the `getLength()` function returns the packet length — for incoming messages the functions `getAddress()` and `getPort()` are used to determine the source host and port number. The `DatagramSocket` class is used to send and receive datagram packets — by default the constructor creates a socket bound to any available port on the local machine but it is possible to specify a particular port number. The `send()` and `receive()` functions accept a DatagramPacket parameter — the receive() function blocks until a packet arrives. The DatagramSocket class close() function is usually called to close a socket but the finalizer ensures that this action is carried out.

The ServerSocket and Socket classes respectively implement server and client sockets — typically, a server application opens a server socket and then waits until a client applet connects to it using a client socket. The ServerSocket constructor binds to a specific local port or (given a port number of zero) to any free port — the constructor also sets up a queue to hold incoming connection requests that cannot be processed immediately. The ServerSocket class accept() function is called to receive incoming connections — the function blocks until a connection is made and then returns a Socket object which can be used to continue the newly formed connection. The server socket can return to listening for another connection request or it can be closed using the ServerSocket class close() function. At the other end of the connection, a client socket is created using the Socket class — the Socket constructor accepts the name or IP address of the server machine and the port number being used by the server application. The Socket class functions getInetAddress() and getPort() return values for the remote end of the connection — the getLocalPort() returns the local port number. The getInputStream() and getOutputStream() functions respectively provide InputStream and OutputStream objects for reading from or writing to the socket. Finally, the Socket class close() function is used to close the socket whenever it is no longer required.

14.6 Summary

The World Wide Web is formed from a collection of Web pages (typically HTML documents) that are interconnected by a series of hyperlinks — a Web browser allows the user to move easily from one document to the next simply by clicking the mouse on the hot-spot associated with a particular hyperlink. Each HTML document consists of a series of elements comprising start and end tags wrapped around some enclosed text. The HTML element contains the HEAD and BODY elments — the HEAD element acts as the document header and contains the TITLE element whilst the BODY element holds the contents of the document. In particular, the APPLET element can appear within the BODY element to embed an applet within a Web page. The APPLET element uses the CODE attribute to provide the applet's class name and the NAME attribute to identify the various applets within a document to the AppletContext interface getApplet() function — the WIDTH and HEIGHT attributes indicate the initial size of the applet within the Web browser. An applet can be customized using various PARAMETER elements nested within the APPLET element — the NAME and VALUE attributes of each PARAMETER element define parameter name and value strings for use with the Applet class getParameter() function. The getAppletInfo() and getParameterInfo() functions allow the user of an applet to obtain information about the applet itself and the parameters which it understands. An applet is started automatically whenever its Web page is first visited and the applet receives calls to its init() and start() functions. The applet functions stop() and start() may then be called any number of times as the applet is deactivated and reactivated by the browser — this happens whenever the user moves away from the applet's Web page and later returns. Eventually the applet will be discarded but before it is its stop() function is called a final time followed by its destroy() function. An applet can display information in the browser's status bar using the Applet class showStatus() function and can request that a new Web page be displayed by calling the AppletContext interface showDocument() function — the Applet class function getAppletContext() returns an AppleContext reference. The Applet class also provides getImage(), getAudioClip() and play() functions to support the straightforward use of images and audio clips — there are also AudioClip interface functions play(), loop() and stop(). The Applet class getCodeBase() function may be used to locate resources stored in sub-directories of the applet directory — the getDocumentBase() function returns the URL of the applet's document. More general resources can be located using the URL and URLConnection classes from the java.net package — the getContent() functions retrieve a pre-constructed object from the resource whilst the openStream() function allows raw data to be read from the resource. The java.net class also defines several classes to support low-level Internet communications — in particular, the InetAddress class encapsulates an IP address. The DatagramPacket and DatagramSocket classes are used to implement a datagram protocol service whilst the ServerSocket and Socket classes respectively represent server and client sockets for a connected stream protocol.